When Treating
All the Kids
the **SAME** Is
the **REAL** Problem

When Treating All the Kids the **SAME** Is the **REAL** Problem

---

Educational Leadership and
the 21st Century Dilemma of Difference

Kendra Johnson

Lisa Williams

CORWIN
A SAGE Company

A SAGE Company

FOR INFORMATION:

Corwin

A SAGE Company

2455 Teller Road

Thousand Oaks, California 91320

(800) 233-9936

www.corwin.com

SAGE Publications Ltd.

1 Oliver's Yard

55 City Road

London, EC1Y 1SP

United Kingdom

SAGE Publications India Pvt. Ltd.

B 1/I 1 Mohan Cooperative Industrial Area

Mathura Road, New Delhi 110 044

India

SAGE Publications Asia-Pacific Pte. Ltd.

3 Church Street

#10–04 Samsung Hub

Singapore 049483

Acquisitions Editor: Dan Alpert

Associate Editor: Kimberly Greenberg

Editorial Assistant: Cesar Reyes

Production Editor: Veronica Stapleton Hooper

Copy Editor: Amy Marks

Typesetter: Hurix Systems Pvt. Ltd.

Proofreader: Sarah J. Duffy

Indexer: Sheila Bodell

Cover Designer: Michael Dubowe

Marketing Manager: Stephanie Trkay

Printed in the United States of America

Library of Congress Cataloging-in-Publication Data

Johnson, Kendra V. (Kendra Vernelle), 1974-
When treating all the kids the same is the real problem: educational leadership and the 21st century dilemma of difference / Kendra Johnson, Lisa Williams.

pages cm.
Includes bibliographical references and index.

ISBN 978-1-4522-8696-9 (alk. paper)

1. Educational equalization—United States.
2. Culturally relevant pedagogy—United States.
3. Children with social disabilites—Education—United States. 4. Educational leadership—United States. I. Title.

LC213.2.J62 2015
379.260973—dc23   2014023506

This book is printed on acid-free paper.

14 15 16 17 18 10 9 8 7 6 5 4 3 2 1

Contents

Acknowledgments

There have been many who have been gracious enough to gift us with experiences that frame the ideas in this book. To all who have crossed our paths and influenced our work, we carry your insights with us every day. We are thankful to our mentors, fellow educators, undergraduate and graduate professors, and numerous voices we encounter in our daily walk that challenge our thinking, ideas, and understanding of what is needed for *each* student to be academically and emotionally successful.

All students enter school full of potential and with dreams about who they will become. If we are willing to notice, listen, and learn, they will teach us so much about who we are and what they need to thrive . . . to become. It is the voices, hopes, and dreams of these young people that led us to this work. We honor the young people who have taught us to honor how they show up to school daily. By acknowledging these lessons learned from students, we know more about how to understand, how we should engage, how we relate, and how we use students' talents as strategic entry points to ensure that each student has a rigorous educational experience every day.

We want to thank our families for their support and encouragement. We hold our grandparents and parents, in particular, in the highest regard: Andrew Jefferson, Doris Jefferson, Lynell Miliam, Andrea Miliam, Jerry Brinkley, Charles Madison, Elijah Lott, Vernelle Lott, Terry Pearson, and Mary Pearson. Of course, there is nothing like a great group of friends who serve as a cheering squad. And we certainly are the beneficiaries of such a team. We want to thank our editor, Dan Alpert, who supported us tirelessly through every phase of this project. He has celebrated our work, while challenging us to refine and reflect to ensure that our work is accessible to all. For this championing of our work, we are indebted.

The Authors' Voices

Dr. Kendra Johnson, Esq.

I recently assumed the role of chief academic officer for Trenton Public Schools in New Jersey (July 2014). While I am also a licensed attorney in the states of Maryland and New Jersey, I consider myself a career educator, having served as classroom teacher, department chairperson, assistant principal, principal, director of Title I, instructional director, chief academic and innovation officer, and adjunct college professor over my seventeen-year career in public education. I have expertise in the areas of school reform and transformation and school improvement. Furthermore, I provided legal advocacy for the parents of students with disabilities and those facing inequitable disciplinary consequences. To that end, I see myself as a visionary leader in urban education because I am convinced that education is the vehicle by which many underserved student groups will realize social mobility. I also believe that education will enable those same students to claim a productive and influential role in making their future—and their children's future—a better one.

My personal journey growing up in a small, racially divided, and socioeconomically challenged midwestern town where there were seven elementary schools, three middle schools, and one high school significantly shapes my outlook today. The idea that daily high-quality instruction is the pathway out of poverty only for urban school students is an idea I challenge. Instead, I contend that daily high-quality instruction is the pathway out of poverty for *any* rural, suburban, and/or urban student.

Dr. Lisa Williams

I am the director of equity and cultural proficiency for the Baltimore County Public Schools. Like Kendra, I, too, am a career educator, having served as classroom teacher, teacher mentor, Title I director, adjunct college professor, and educational consultant. I have expertise in culturally responsive instruction, creating equitable schools and school districts, and school transformation. Furthermore, I support schools in implementing innovative initiatives that are designed to accelerate the achievement of underserved students. I believe that a quality educational experience is the linchpin to social and economic mobility. It doesn't matter what vocation our students aspire to, there is no getting around the ongoing progress of becoming educated. I believe in and am committed to helping educators make this journey a meaningful one for young people. I am committed because I know that when education works, teachers and principals don't see generation after generation of the same family in depressed communities. I know that when public education works, teachers and principals do see mothers, fathers, sisters, and brothers come back to depressed communities to serve as partners in the struggle to improve lives. I was born in Baltimore and attended Baltimore City Public Schools. My own journey is a testament to what can happen when just one child is educated. Education continues to help me evolve into my own humanity and into the humanity of others. It is from this personal and professional space that the ideas in this book resonate for me.

Dr. Kendra Johnson, Esq., and Dr. Lisa Williams

We began our careers together at a Title I school in Baltimore City Public Schools. It was there that we met and began to forge a long-lasting commitment to doing more for marginalized students. We realized even then that, in many instances, diverse students relied exclusively on us as educators to create bridges to better life options by providing a quality instructional program every day. After some years, we both left this Title I school; however, our walks remained focused on equity and access to a quality instructional program. Professionally, our walks crossed again in the early 2000s in Baltimore County Public Schools. In our respective roles, we worked jointly on several school transformation initiatives within public schools through grant programs like Race to the Top and School Improvement, as well as on older improvement initiatives like the Comprehensive School Reform Demonstration Grant program. It is through these experiences that we developed the experiential base undergirding this book.

Introduction

The names on the desks tell the story of the changing face of public education. In previous years, James sat next to Eddie. Now, Mohan and Malik sit in those desks. Furthermore, Susie and Mary are sitting next to Mariana and Zari. Our classrooms are continuing to change. The education community must both face and respond to this reality. The public education system in the United States serves the majority of all school-aged children—49.5 million of 55.3 million children—but the majority of those children are no longer white, middle-class, suburban and rural students (Aud et al., 2012). The following data illustrate this point:

- Between 1990 and 2010, the percentage of white students in the nation's public schools decreased from 29 percent to 27.7 percent and has been decreasing steadily since (Aud et al., 2012).
- In 2010, 20 percent of students attended high-poverty elementary and secondary schools (Aud et al., 2012).
- In 2009, 21 percent of students spoke a language other than English at home (Aud et al., 2011).
- In 2010, approximately 13 percent of public school students received educational supports authorized by the Individuals with Disabilities Act (IDEA; Aud et al., 2012).
- One in four public school students is from a home headed by a single parent (Federal Interagency Forum on Child and Family Statistics, 2013).

These data suggest significant cultural implications for teaching and learning. They also suggest that educators must immediately and continually examine whether each student has equitable access to daily quality instruction. The critical questions are: What does it mean to create a culturally responsive learning environment that makes access to high academic outcomes a possibility for each student? And, as leaders, how do we move our school communities forward in ways that respond to these changes? The answers to these questions require us to think differently about how we conduct the process of schooling. The reality is that we must address the changes needed in public education. Our student population is not simply *going to* become more diverse; that diversity is already here! As educators, we must find the lens and perspective that allow us to make instructional decisions that reflect the learning needs of our students. We were inspired to write this book with that imperative in mind.

WHY READ THIS BOOK?

We break with the conventional wisdom that numbers rule and technical solutions (those that are quick, known, and finite) are sufficient. Effective teaching can be assessed only insofar as it is described by students' demonstrated learning. Therefore, we embrace adaptive, process-oriented thinking as the blueprint for addressing challenges in educational equity and access. We embrace synthesizing findings from both research-based and evidence-based practice as the beginning points for school transformation toward equity. Engaging in equity-focused leadership is, in part, a commitment to personal transformation. It requires each of us to reflect on personal beliefs and behaviors that drive the outcomes. Because a major part of this work is personal, we do not rely solely on empirical practice. We believe that transformation toward equity requires the leader to accept the challenge to change and then become a change agent. This book is a synthesis of educational research on topics ranging from scheduling theory to change management and change leadership, from addressing educational equity as practice to developing transformed school practice. Since we aim to equip the users of this book with a framework and a process to defy the predictable patterns of underperformance of diverse student groups, we emphasize *leadership for equity that ensures students have access to daily quality instruction.*

According to Heifetz, Linsky, and Grashow (2009), "adaptive leadership is the practice of mobilizing people to tackle tough challenges and thrive" (p. 14). It involves understanding what about an organization should be maintained and what should be changed. The skill of adaptive leadership is precisely what is needed to lead schools and organizations serving large populations of diverse students when the goal is high achievement outcomes for each learner. Adaptive challenges, like those characterizing the disparities in student outcomes, can be tackled only as we change our priorities, beliefs, and practices (Heifetz et al., 2009). Adaptive leadership requires passion, persistence, and process—all of which we examine in this book through the lens of our collective experience at all levels of the public school system organization. It is the combination of passion, persistence, and process that can transform outcomes; possessing one without the others is insufficient to unearth and address the reasons for the stubborn gaps in outcomes that plague the public education system (Singleton & Linton, 2006).

Our current educational culture is rife with strategies, initiatives, and programs aimed at our diverse student groups. However, through this book, we want to suggest that a fundamentally different course of action is needed. The cultural implications of demographic changes in the public school population are significant. Diversity in the student and community population means, in part, that they will offer varied ways of understanding and experiencing the world. These differences should influence how we organize for teaching and learning. Responding practically to the challenges in serving a diverse population (within an institution not designed with diversity in mind) means that we as educators must focus on equity and the process we use must examine outcomes, not intentions. In this book, we urge readers to gain entry points to this work through the PACE Framework (Figure 0.1).

PACE represents the process component of the passion, persistence, and process trifecta. Through PACE, we ask the leader to begin with his or her instructional vision for equity. We ask, "What do you personally believe about educational equity, and what does it look like to you when it's happening in teaching and learning?" and "What do data and research for your school population tell you?"

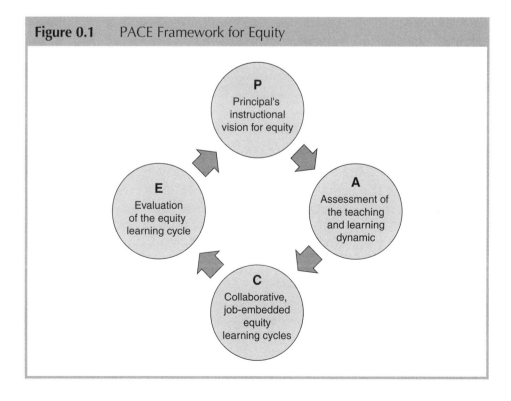

Figure 0.1 PACE Framework for Equity

The answers to these questions must use specific and intentional language. From that instructional vision for equity, the leader then assesses teaching and learning; that assessment combined with ongoing equity cycles helps to determine growth and development opportunities, which are analyzed against student outcomes and the vision for equity. The PACE Framework allows for both the depth and the breadth of analysis that leaders need to employ to eliminate gaps in student outcomes. Naming, confronting, embracing, and then addressing the "truth" as revealed by data are integral pieces of this work. No longer can we explain away the inequities in access to high-quality instruction by saying, "we are doing our best," or "these data are good, considering our demographics," or "we just do not have enough materials [books/people, etc.]."

Consider how the diversity of your student population influences the teaching and learning in your organization. What can you identify? Without a framework that (a) uses equity as the lens and (b) includes a process that evaluates outcomes, how many strategies are you implementing that are truly moving your school community away from the predictability of demographics?

EMBRACING A NEW FRAMEWORK: MOVING AWAY FROM *MINORITY* STUDENT CONSIDERATIONS

Changes in our public school population require our collective, strategic reconsideration and reorganization in service of all students. As in the larger society, the idea of *minority* takes on a full range of meaning and is complex. In the field of education, the term *minority* includes but is not limited to numerical, racial, cultural, ethnic, and linguistic connotations. More important, as we seek to understand the needs of the learners we have traditionally considered *minority*, what are the implications of the operational definition we choose? In education, we often use that term as a code for black and brown children, poor children, city children. The term itself suggests that marginalizing these populations is reasonable simply because they are not high in number. However, as students with these characteristics become the majority groups in public schools around the country, we need to replace the coded language. Race and ethnicity are two major factors of diversity, but they intersect with myriad other factors that, as culturally competent educators, we should understand.

Perhaps the more useful descriptors going forward into the twenty-first century are those that describe more accurately the teaching and learning challenges for the learners we serve today. One thing is clear—we need to describe accurately and know clearly who our clients are. Consider how this plays out in practice for one elementary school principal.

In creating her staffing plan, an elementary school principal was strug-gling with how to allocate one position between two areas of need. She wanted to involve all stakeholders, so she had planning conversations with teachers, parents, and student representatives. She reviewed the data and shared the results with the stakeholders. The dilemma was whether to add a teacher to fourth grade and decrease class sizes in that grade, which would open on the first day of school with twenty-seven students, or to fund an additional reading specialist to work on acceleration because reading achievement was stagnant. The parents and teachers advocated for hiring an additional fourth-grade teacher because they believed that the reading achievement stagnation was due to a lack of parental involvement. The principal, however, knew that the demographic changes in the student population were creating challenges for teachers who relied on past practice rather than on culturally responsive practice. The data from her analysis were clear: As the population was becom-ing more diverse racially, economically, and linguistically, reading achieve-ment had become flat. The principal was concerned that if this academic performance trend was not addressed aggressively, student achievement would start to decline. The school would then be dealing with a whole host of different issues. The principal clearly saw the benefit of hiring a teacher to work on accelerating achievement for struggling students and building capacity for all teachers, even if the parents—and other educators—did not.

When we continue to use terms like *minority* without challenging our thinking and assumptions, we are less critical of standing policies, practices, and procedures. As a result, "too often, attitudes and beliefs that contrib-ute to the normalization of failure are unchallenged, and when failure is normalized, educators often grow comfortable seeing minority students underperform and fail in large number" (Boykin & Noguera, 2011, p. 31).

Most educators—even most people generally—probably are familiar with the bell curve. Figure 0.2 displays graphically our col-lective expectation for the "normal" distribution of performance most often associated with test performance in public education.

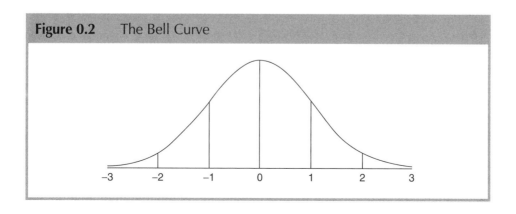

Figure 0.2   The Bell Curve

The figure predicts that the majority of students (70 percent of them) will perform in the average range, while approximately 15 percent of students will score in each of the high and low ends of an assessment (Warne, Godwin, & Smith, 2013). This predictive model has powerful implications for how we respond to performance patterns in public schools.

The bell curve, by its very nature, accepts the fact that some students will achieve at a higher rate and allows us to accept that some students will not achieve. It seems natural, even logical, to accept that not all students will succeed at everything they try. The insidious nature of this belief, though, is that in the minds of many in our society, there is a strong pairing of *minority* students and underachievement. As a result, the bell curve takes on a different meaning. The demographic predictability of low achievement, as well as bell-curve thinking, gives us license to shrug our shoulders and say that there are just *those* students—the ones in the left-hand tail of the curve—who will underachieve no matter what we do. The central work of the twenty-first-century educator is to transform the public school into an institution that defies the typical presumptions of achievement present in the bell curve. Assessing student performance at quarterly benchmarks or during yearly accountability testing is not sufficient to eliminate gaps and prepare students. Bringing about high outcomes for each student requires daily consideration and assessment. The critical question is: How does a school leader create conditions that allow underserved students to defy historical demographic predictability?

Leaders who seek to achieve educational equity begin by recognizing that many public education practices (including those done out of habit, those carried out in the belief that they are "best practice," or those that are simply district or school policies) do not meet the needs of students attending our schools today. Serving a diverse student population requires leaders to seek answers and processes in nontraditional places.

Students themselves are the most powerful source of information. Seeking information from students may seem simple, but the legacy of marginalization and low expectations makes it difficult for adults to truly consider students' voices. Responding to the learning needs of *each* student through effective instructional practice is the challenge. Daily instructional practices in teaching and learning are critical influencers in eliminating achievement gaps and in ensuring that students are prepared for life beyond K–12. Creating a school culture in which school leaders use real-time data to determine the effectiveness of daily teaching and learning practices is the means to serving a diverse student population. Forward-thinking leaders create a paradigm to develop classroom practices that can be used to educate each student.

Leaders do this work by creating conditions that enable school staff to assess students' access to daily quality instruction. The PACE Framework is the structure through which a school community or school district can realize the goal of quality daily instruction for each student. PACE is a thinking map that guides school leaders through their daily work while allowing them to prioritize equity. The PACE Framework was named in a deliberate attempt to maintain focus on the critical importance of equity-focused instructional leadership in advancing schools in the work of transformed practice.

We wrote this book with this data-driven, student-centered, and equity-focused objective in mind. Demographic changes in our student population require each of us to reconsider and reconceive daily teaching and learning practices in a manner that will help each student to achieve high outcomes. We want our readers to ask, "What course of action do *I* need to take to meet the learning needs of a significantly changed public school population?"

THE URGENCY TO CONFRONT THE DILEMMAS IN TEACHING AND LEARNING

As career educators working in public school districts that serve large and diverse populations, we know that managing difference in an educational culture of increasing standardization is especially difficult. Identifying effective instructional strategies for diverse groups of students is also challenging. Educators who want to improve outcomes for marginalized students in such an environment must ask themselves critical questions, including "*Whom* are we talking about when we describe a policy, a practice, a strategy, or an intervention as effective?" and "What factors must we consider about our students, today and in the future, before we adjust our instructional practices?"

The first question creates a powerful focal point for school leaders who are addressing the challenges of the demographic shift and its impact on teaching and learning. One need only examine the achievement patterns of rural and urban students, poor students, students receiving special education services, English language learners, and/or racially diverse students across the country to see that traditional assumptions about teaching and learning fail to address the needs of every group of students.

In response to the second question, school leaders who create environments in which the chronic underperformance of diverse students is not an accepted norm deliberately challenge the instructional environment. Instead they ask, "Is what we are doing working for *each student?*" If the answer to that question is no, then these leaders adjust instructional practices to get to yes. Therein lies their strength and value as equity-focused instructional leaders. Creating the necessary changes in systems, structures, practices, and policies is central to these educators' daily work.

WHO SHOULD READ THIS BOOK?

We wrote this book with six readers in mind: principals; aspiring principals; educational leaders charged with building principals' capacity; educational leaders who write policy; educational leaders who write curriculum and support the implementation of the curriculum with fidelity; and other educational leaders charged with supporting the work of school communities. In this book, we explore the leadership challenges of responding to America's changing public school population. More specifically, we address the equity-focused instructional leadership necessary to ensure that each student has access to high-quality teaching and learning. In short, we examine the leadership imperative for those pursuing educational equity. Education stakeholders at all levels may find this book informative, but those who guide and direct school operations will find it most useful. This book is based on literature describing the principal as the greatest influence on teaching and learning in a school (Louis et al., 2010). What gets done in a school is what the leader sets as a priority. School leaders can translate quality instructional *priorities* into quality instructional *practices.* The transformation to quality instruction for each student begins once the school leader has decided to make this transformation the school's top priority.

We wrote this book with the practitioner in mind. As such, the chapters describe the narrative critical in transforming a school or district from the very first engagement with the topic to advanced engagement in institutionalizing practices, policies, and procedures that support equitable achievement outcomes. We examine the imperative to pursue equity in the beginning of the book. Why? Experience has shown us that intellectual knowledge of the achievement gap is not enough to convince a community to pursue equity, so early on we examine the moral imperative and the complexity of social issues related to the under-preparation of young people. We then examine past practice (school reform) to offer perspective on the limitations of our constant pursuit of technical solutions (those that are quick and known) as we endeavor to respond in practice to achievement disparities. In the rest of the book, we describe the process and adaptive practice. We examine adaptive practice in situations that occur in schools across the country every day to offer insights into how one might advance an equity agenda. Reading the chapters in order will allow the leader to move his or her team methodically into deep engagement with educational equity work.

HOW IS THE BOOK ORGANIZED?

This book is divided into three parts. Part I gives readers the context for understanding why we need to change the paradigm that guides teaching and learning and leadership to better address each student's learning needs. We explain how the traditional organization of schooling excludes consideration of factors that are central when serving a diverse student body. This section equips leaders with the explanation they need to help their school communities understand why school *transformation* and not school improvement is necessary. The section concludes with a description of the PACE Framework, our research- and evidence-based process designed to guide efforts toward high, equitable academic outcomes.

Part II examines how a leader might apply the PACE Framework to advance equity-focused instructional leadership to ensure students' access to daily, high-quality teaching and learning. What makes the PACE Framework unique is that we offer a means for addressing equity and teaching and learning as a natural part of the decisions that leaders make in schools every day. Far too often, "equity work" is an add-on, a supplement. In those instances, we make decisions about the whole school and then we consider equity—if equity is considered at all. We know from experience that the frenetic pace of activity in the schoolhouse is only heightening and that add-on equity does not work. In response to this, in Part II, we provide practical examples of how PACE can be applied in typical situations and decisions. We take readers through the PACE implementation process, identifying the critical elements that keep staff focused on equity. We call these critical elements *Principled Practices.* In working on educational equity at all levels of the public school organization—classroom, school, central office, and senior leadership—we try to help leaders to maintain their focus on practices that will make a difference.

Finally, Part III examines how schools and districts can institutionalize the PACE Framework so that they are able to respond to twenty-first-century learning changes. The changing student demographic serves as the focal point of why we need a dynamic framework guiding teaching and learning. It is just as important to recognize that the changing global marketplace, the changing sociocultural structure, and the influence of technology will affect our ability to achieve equitable outcomes. Institutionalizing PACE is about institutionalizing both lens and process to keep the school in productive motion.

In writing *When Treating All the Kids the SAME Is the REAL Problem*, we hoped to invoke intense thought, reflection, and action regarding equity-focused instructional leadership. Accordingly, we wrote this book to assist readers in considering their own contexts as they lead their schools toward high academic outcomes for each student. Data across the country, from school to school, and from district to district, reveal that we can no longer treat all kids the same but expect different outcomes for students who have day after day, month after month, and year and year consistently underperformed. Each chapter includes features designed to enable internal examination of the inputs that are driving the outcomes in a school or school system. The subtlety of the decisions and actions that maintains and perpetuates inequity cannot be understood, identified, or responded to without reflection, analysis, and perspective seeking. As a result, we provide reflective questions, discussion questions, practical implementation tools, and guiding questions and statements to prompt the examination of school practices. These embedded resources are designed to guide readers through the deep consideration or, in some cases, deliberate action critical to the transformation process. Leadership teams may use these tools to guide discussions, or leaders may find them useful for professional development. Although partnering with other schools or districts that are pursuing educational equity can be useful, simply adopting practices that are working on other campuses is not sufficient to interrupt patterns of demographically predictable underperformance.

Data show that we can no longer follow traditional ways of teaching and learning, particularly when what we have been doing for *all* is failing *some* of our students. For those committed to the moral, social, and economic imperatives of serving each student at a high level, this book provides a responsive, systematic guide for data-driven decision making that will help meet the needs of the *some* as well as the *all*.

Part I
The Context

1

Why Is Treating All Students the Same the Real Problem?

All animals are equal, but some animals are more equal than others.

—*Animal Farm* (Orwell, 1945, p. 133)

The foundation of American democracy is the ability of individuals, at least in theory, to move between social classes or occupational groups based on their knowledge, ability, and commitment, regardless of their social position in childhood. Social mobility is defined as "the movement or opportunities for movement between different social classes or occupational groups" (Aldridge, 2003, p. 189). Some observers would suggest that socioeconomic mobility is facilitated by marriage, family affiliation, political power, and more, but as Horace Mann said more than 150 years ago, education "beyond all other devices of human origin, is the great equalizer of the conditions of men, the balance-wheel of the social machinery." According to Mann (1948), public schools are the linchpin of American democracy, ultimately giving poor children the possibility of socioeconomic mobility.

With compulsory education laws in all fifty states, education is a readily available opportunity. A quality education gives access to the promise of the American dream. Education, the one variable that can help *any* individual advance, is within reach. Unfortunately, high-quality daily instruction is not available to every student. For years, schools embraced mission statements focused on treating all students the same. Leaders often say, "All means all," or "Our schools are places where *all* students are successful." Our response to these and similar statements is simple: "How has living the world of 'all means all' served our most traditionally underserved populations? Do we no longer have achievement, opportunity, and/or expectation gaps?" We acknowledge the good intentions behind making the same resources available to all students in order to promote academic success. But a shift in thinking is required if we are to realize the levels of achievement needed to eliminate achievement, opportunity, and expectation gaps. Hence, the idea of moving from equality to equity undergirds the statement that "treating all the kids the same is the real problem." The failure to educate each child equitably has an adverse impact locally as well as globally.

At the local level, high unemployment rates and low income levels contribute to great disparities among various racial groups. When citizens are unable to pay local taxes, in particular, property taxes, local governments become unable to fund public schools fully since the majority of public school funding is based on local property taxes. Local economics contribute directly to the ability of some communities to contribute more funds for public schools than other communities (U.S. Department of Education, National Center for Education Statistics, n.d.). The unequal nature of public school funding across the United States is not the subject of this book; however, each student should be educated well so that he or she can become a productive, tax-paying citizen in his or her chosen community.

At the global level, according to the Organization for Economic Co-operation and Development, fifteen-year-old students from the United States rank seventeenth in the world in science and twenty-fifth in math. In addition, in college graduation rates, the United States ranks twelfth among developed countries, a drop in rank from number one just a few decades ago. U.S. elementary schools are ranked seventy-ninth in enrollment. The U.S. educational infrastructure is ranked twenty-third in the world, well behind the world's progressive economies (Aud et al., 2011; Zakaria, 2011). As the nation's student population has grown increasingly diverse, the United States has struggled to maintain its foothold on the mountain peak of top performance, highlighting the need for educational practices that will help the nation return to a position of global power. U.S. Secretary of Education Arne Duncan referred to the current quality of public schools and the need for equal access to effective instruction as "the civil rights issue of our times" (Price, 2011, p. 1).

THE TRANSFORMATIVE IMPERATIVE OF EDUCATION TO MOVE FROM EDUCATING ALL TO EDUCATING EACH STUDENT IN THE TWENTY-FIRST CENTURY

An increasingly competitive global environment demands that we graduate *each* student prepared to enter the adult world—whether that is college (two-year programs, four-year programs, and certificate programs), an immediate career beyond high school, or the military. Taken collectively, these issues provide the backdrop for equity work. To transform—not simply repair—public education so that it can respond effectively to the academic, social, and behavioral needs of each student, we must work with today's students in the presence of the complex conditions that impact their lives. Educators must live in the question, "What are we doing to create a space for each student to become a critical thinker, a social change agent, a masterful scientist, or a future doctor?" Educators must give students opportunities so that their generation's innovative leaders can develop and emerge, like Dr. Martin Luther King, Steve Jobs, and Albert Einstein before them. Furthermore, educators must make a concerted effort to explore the characteristics of a twenty-first-century learner and to scaffold those skills into the daily instructional program.

In many school districts, diverse students are identified too frequently as being in need of intervention. The rush to intervene, remediate, or accelerate often clouds what should be the first question: Does each student, irrespective of demographics, have *access* to a quality core instructional program? As public school educators, do we really want the United States to become an "intervention nation," as our public schools become blacker, browner, poorer, and more linguistically diverse? As we attempt to respond to the relevant variables in teaching and learning today, does it make sense that our structures, from the most basic to the most sophisticated, fail to serve each student? Does your school's frame of reference for instructional decision making represent conditions that either no longer exist or are more the exception than the rule (such as teaching students who "sit and get," adequately preparing only the most able, using technology ineffectively or not at all)?

The urgency is obvious when we identify who is served by America's public education system. The pattern becomes evident when we identify who is represented in the lower socioeconomic and under-educated groups. The 2010 U.S. Census, for instance, revealed that non-white groups had lower mean incomes than whites. For example, at $50,673, white Americans' mean annual income was approximately $20,000 higher than that of African Americans, at $31,969.

Figure 1.1 Median Annual Earnings of Full-Time, Full-Year Wage and Salary Workers Ages 25 and Older, by Educational Attainment, Sex, and Race/Ethnicity: 2007

Sex and Race/ Ethnicity	Educational Attainment						
	Less than high school completion	HS completion	Some college, no degree	Associate's degree	Bachelor's degree	Master's degree	Doctorate or first professional degree
Total	$25,000	$32,000	$38,000	$41,700	$53,000	$62,000	$ 86,000
Male							
White	28,000	37,200	45,000	49,000	61,000	75,000	100,000
Black	32,000	40,000	47,000	50,000	65,000	75,500	100,000
Hispanic	27,000	32,000	37,000	41,000	50,000	60,000	95,000
Asian	25,000	30,000	38,000	42,000	50,000	68,000	85,000
Native Hawaiian, Pacific Islander	++	++	++	++	++	++	++
American Indian/ Alaska Native	++	35,000	++	++	++	++	++
Two or more races	++	30,000	39,000	++	76,500	++	++
Female							
White	20,000	27,000	33,000	35,800	45,000	55,000	70,000
Black	20,800	29,000	34,000	38,000	46,000	55,000	65,400
Hispanic	20,000	25,000	30,000	33,000	42,000	55,000	++
Asian	18,200	25,000	31,000	32,500	40,000	52,500	65,500
Native Hawaiian, Pacific Islander	++	++	++	++	++	++	++
American Indian, Alaska Native	++	++	++	++	++	++	++
Two or more races	++	26,500	32,900	++	++	++	++

++ Reporting standards not met

Source: U.S. Department of Commerce (2010).

Even when white Americans and African Americans have similar incomes, data describing the wealth gap (such as artifacts of past discriminatory practices, including housing and employment) reveal a disturbing pattern. According to a Pew Research (2011) report, the wealth ratio for whites to African Americans is twenty to one and the ratio for whites to Hispanics is eighteen to one (see also Figure 1.1).

A quality education provides individuals with an opportunity to obtain adequate employment and to amass wealth. Therefore, our work as educators has far greater implications than we often realize. Whatever a person's economic status, race, religion, or native language, education is an essential component of establishing that individual's professional status. Employers screen applicants and base their salaries on the degrees they have earned and the professional certificates they have. Those with a bachelor's degree or a more advanced degree earn significantly higher salaries than those with less education (U.S. Department of Commerce, 2008). As illustrated in Figure 1.1, the more education an individual possesses, the more potential he or she has for positive economic positioning.

Educators must have the courage to enhance systems, structures, practices, and policies to provide ample support *ahead* of the need so that intervention will not be inevitable for diverse students. The work of transformation requires a practical, job-embedded framework that can be a win-win for all stakeholders.

CONFRONTING THE DILEMMA OF DIFFERENCE

The dilemma of difference, a phrase coined by Harvard Law School dean Martha Minow, is used to frame the case for educating each student well (Yudof, Levin, Moran, Ryan, & Bowman, 2012). The dilemma of difference refers to the uncertainty individuals experience when they attempt to determine whether "groups should conform to a single norm or preserve their differences in a pluralistic society" (Yudof et al., 2012, p. 663). Educators often try to honor student differences while maintaining the same rigor for all. In the effort to honor differences, educators are often met with a concern that the "law, although trying to eradicate inequality, will simply entrench students' differences" (p. 663). A larger context encourages individuals to embrace the idea of *color blindness.* From a historical perspective, we acknowledge that the idea of being color blind may have been helpful to address race relations. However, the thinking associated with color blindness will only contribute to the ongoing dilemma of figuring out how to serve each student well.

The dilemma of difference requires (a) contending with daily teaching and learning at the classroom level and (b) intervening in teacher and student interactions so that students are met at their instructional levels and encouraged, supported, and taught until they are able to reach globally competitive standards. School leaders, as the most powerful influencers of teaching and learning practices (Blasé & Roberts, 1994), must address differences in achievement by analyzing students' daily access to quality instruction. Teachers' instructional practices and the learning opportunities they provide students, along with the support of principals and district central office personnel, are the infrastructure for equity. To confront the dilemma of difference, school leaders must take an equity-focused instructional leadership stance in which the assessment *for* learning drives the work of the school. If conversations and decisions about how to improve achievement for diverse students do not change the school's instructional program, then student performance is unlikely to be affected. The optimal framework for achieving educational equity focuses on using student outcomes to drive school decisions and the practices that follow.

The example of Alison Brooks illustrates this principle. Brooks was appointed principal of a high school with a large number of students receiving English language services. As she began her work, Brooks found that a majority of the students with English language needs were performing the lowest on state assessments and often were taking longer than four years to graduate from high school. When she sat down with the school's eleventh-grade team leader, their conversation illustrated the dilemma of difference:

Eleventh-grade team leader: Welcome to the school, Ms. Brooks. We're glad you're here. We have some scheduling adjustments that need to be made. The eleventh-grade teachers met with the tenth-grade team during end-of-the-year transition meetings and discussed the low performance of students requiring English language services. The tenth-grade teachers believe keeping all students with English language needs together in one classroom is appropriate so their language needs will not interfere with other students (for example, in group discussions) or interfere with the teachers' ability to plan high-quality instruction due to the language needs of students. They also believe that we need to adjust the students' schedules to put all students with English language needs together in one classroom. By doing so, teachers will only have to prepare one lesson a day with significant academic language focus. Our team is worried about the classroom dynamics of all classes if we don't make any changes.

Principal Brooks: Help me understand how the original schedule was created. What factors did you use to place the students?

Eleventh-grade team leader: Originally, we grouped the students based on their content needs using end-of-course assessment data from grade ten.

Principal Brooks: If students were grouped based on their end-of-course assessments, why would you want to regroup them based on their English language needs? If students were able to perform on the end-of-course assessments and were subsequently placed according to those data, why would we disregard the data and regroup them based solely on students' needs for English language services? Apparently, some students with English language needs are performing at or above grade level on end-of-course assessments. Let's discuss the instructional needs of each student. Then we can have an informed discussion about possible class changes.

Like Brooks, school leaders frequently have to determine when to consider students' differences in instructional decisions. In this case, the difference was students' needs for English language services. Most readers will likely respond to the preceding exchange by saying, "Of course you would allow students' end-of-year assessment data to drive course placement." However, some educators are conflicted when confronted with students' differences. In this instance, the need for English language services is the difference, and the point of conflict is how to best meet students' needs. Should students needing these services be grouped together to emphasize their English language proficiency development or should other data, like end-of-course assessments, drive student placement? As Brooks and other school leaders contend with the complexities of this work within the context of the school culture, it is critical to acknowledge and address teachers' beliefs about what students and/or student groups can and cannot do. Perhaps the most challenging aspects of a school's culture, which school leaders need to examine, are the hidden beliefs behind teachers' daily interactions with students.

The statements outlined in Figure 1.2 are intended to stimulate your thinking. Do you subscribe to these beliefs? Do your colleagues?

Figure 1.2 What Beliefs Form My Case for Educating Each Student Well?

To frame your thinking, reflect on five essential statements that shape the case for educating each student to a high level:

1. I believe that each and every student should have access to a quality education.
2. I believe that students arrive in school with assets and that educators must embrace an asset-based mindset during the teaching and learning process.
3. I believe that students' successes are, in significant part, due more to their commitment to effort than to their innate ability.
4. I believe that teachers have the ability to help each student develop perseverance and resiliency.
5. I believe that school-based leaders have the ability to create a learning environment that will ensure each student is educated well.

Specifically, consider how your beliefs affect student outcomes. Knowingly or unknowingly, our beliefs impact the practices, protocols, and processes that affect our students' experiences in the classroom. Managing our beliefs affects how we work within school communities and how we establish the space and opportunity needed for each student to be educated well.

A NEW FRAMEWORK FOR EQUITY

Joseph Demp, a principal assigned to an elementary school with a school-wide Title I program, required every grade level to plan a monthly field trip for students in order to compensate for what he perceived as his underprivileged students' lack of exposure to outside experiences. The field trips consumed a significant amount of instructional time, and in a reflection, Demp, through the encouragement of his supervisor, began to assess the value of the trips. The assessment began with Demp's assumption that, because his school was a Title I school, if the school did not give students these experiences, they would not get them at home. The assessment then required Demp to respond to the following questions: What data support that assumption? Did you survey parents or students to find out their experiences? What is the educational purpose of the field trips? How do they relate to the curriculum? Are teachers connecting the trips to previous and future classroom lessons? How are you holding teachers accountable for authentically connecting field trips to the curriculum and classroom instruction?

Demp recognized that he was requiring the trips out of habit, assuming that because of students' socioeconomic status, they needed to take a lot of trips. He realized that he was disregarding instructional time. Upon reflection, he acknowledged that his decisions were based on a false premise and agreed to gather data from teachers and parents. One of the most challenging aspects of equity work is accepting that sometimes, despite good intentions, our beliefs hinder efforts to educate each student well. In this case, the invisible walls limiting access to daily quality instruction were created by the well-intentioned instructional leader.

Figure 1.3 illustrates our Data-Driven, Student-Centered Framework for Achieving Educational Equity, which is designed to help school leaders assess aspects of a school's operation that may very well be invisible to the collective. The framework identifies critical areas that school leaders should monitor in order to achieve high outcomes for each student. It also serves as a conversation starter on educational equity by focusing on student outcomes.

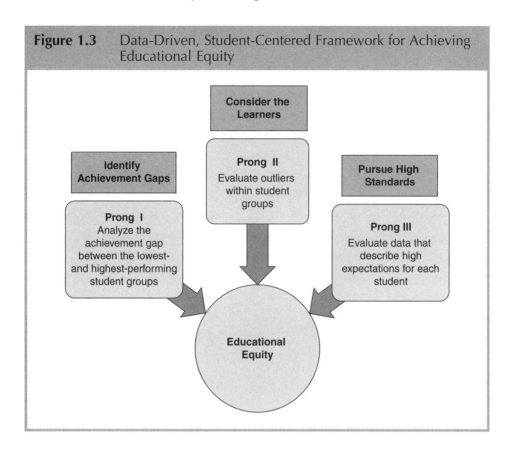

Figure 1.3   Data-Driven, Student-Centered Framework for Achieving Educational Equity

Instructional leaders can use the framework's three central prongs to describe the school's or district's context for equity work: analysis of achievement gaps between and within student groups, focus on individual learners, and progress toward high standards for each student. In each prong, the school community analyzes student achievement and performance trends using at least three years of data. If it is practical to do so, examining performance and achievement data over a longer period will make the identification of trends even clearer. If fewer than three years of data are available, the available information can be used to understand the current state of educational equity.

Prong I prompts the school or district to obtain clear and honest data about the scope of the equity challenge. At this level of analysis, the goal is to use international, national, state, and/or local data to reveal trends. The educational equity picture can be framed using indicators like achievement, participation, suspensions, referrals to special education, and so on. Figure 1.4 provides a template that can be used to show gaps. Data from Figure 1.4 can be displayed using a line graph so that school staff can see the gaps. Notice that data are by race, socioeconomic status, English language learner (ELL) status, and students receiving special education services (SE). Additional student groups should be added as needed to describe the school or district population fully.

Figure 1.4   Identifying Gaps—Data-Driven, Student-Centered Framework Organizational Map

Using Accountability Data (state tests, correlated benchmark assessments, national assessments)*	Student Group	Average Performance			
	Race				
	Participation in the Free and Reduced Meals (FARMS) Program				
	Identified as an English Language Learner (ELL)				
	Receiving Special Education (SE) Services				
Using School Performance Data (quarter/semester grades, interim reports, end-of-course grades, retention rates, promotion rates)*	Student Group	Average Performance			
	Race				
	FARMS				
	ELL				
	SE				
Using Academically Related Data (suspensions, school support teams [SSTs] leading to individual education plans [IEPs], in-school suspensions [ISS], attendance data)*	Student Group	Average Participation			
		Suspension	SST to IEP	ISS	Attendance
	Race				
	FARMS				
	ELL				
	SE				

Note: The listed data sources are examples only; the lists are not exhaustive. Specific data should be selected as appropriate and applicable for grade level.

Critical to engaging in equity work is naming who is experiencing disparities. As such, data must be disaggregated in a manner that enables stakeholders to discuss which students are being underserved.

Prong II of the framework challenges leaders to engage staff in thinking about individual learners while considering the data. The key question is: Who are they? At this stage of analysis, the idea is to explore variations in achievement within student groups and critically analyze outlier students within student groups. Educators can then begin to address the question: How am I adapting my instruction to meet the needs of each student? Prong II focuses the consideration of students' learning needs through the lens of teachers' instructional capacity. These discussions will bring forth examinations of culturally responsive practices. Figure 1.5 illustrates how the data can be organized so that patterns emerge. Depending on the school or district size, leaders can select one grade at a time or analyze a sample of students from each grade. For this analysis, it is important to use student identities—names or even pictures. One helpful hint is to meet in a room large enough to post pictures of students clustered or scattered along the achievement continuum.

Finally, and critically important, in Prong III, leaders in the school or district community examine all students' performance using the lens of high expectations for each learner. This step is critical because it exposes educators' beliefs. We have to know when our beliefs are not aligned with real student outcomes. What we do with that knowledge is the substance of our equity leadership agenda. Prong III allows us to dispel the belief that doing equity work means lowering our standards. In this analysis, leaders use data strategically and objectively to examine the reality of high standards for each student. Ideas such as access to rigor and high standards are commonplace in educational discourse. Less common is an objective examination of whether educators are supporting each student in a manner that makes high outcomes possible. Figure 1.6 offers a structure that school staff can use to examine data through this lens.

The Data-Driven, Student-Centered Framework for Achieving Educational Equity helps educators to analyze student achievement and performance trends to begin the work of transformation. The framework is designed to illuminate differences in achievement experiences among students. To pursue equity, educators must identify, examine, and respond to these differences. The framework moves its users into a state of awareness about the scope of differences within a class, school, or district, and it contains the information from which responses to challenges of equity and access can emerge.

Figure 1.5	Considering the Learners—Data-Driven, Student-Centered Framework Organizational Map				
Using Accountability Data	Student Group	Mean	Median	Mode	Range (lowest–highest)
	Race				
	FARMS				
	ELL				
	SE				
Using School Performance Data	Student Group	Mean	Median	Mode	Range (lowest–highest)
	Race				
	FARMS				
	ELL				
	SE				
Using Academically Related Data	Student Group	Risk Index and Participation			
		Suspension	SST to IEP	ISS	Absent more than 5 days cumulatively
	Race				
	FARMS				
	ELL				
	SE				

Note: See Figure 1.4 for suggested data sources.

Figure 1.6		Pursuing High Standards—Data-Driven, Student-Centered Framework Organizational Map			
Using Accountability Data	Student Group	Percentage of Students Scoring at the Highest Level			
	Race				
	FARMS				
	ELL				
	SE				
Using School Performance Data	Student Group	Number of Students Receiving Grades A and B			
	Race				
	FARMS				
	ELL				
	SE				
Participation in Rigorous Course Offerings	Student Group	Average Participation			
		Gifted and Talented (GT) Enrollment	Advanced Placement (AP) Enrollment	Honors Enrollment	Dual Enrollment
	Race				
	FARMS				
	ELL				
	SE				

MOVING TO A NEW PARADIGM

Few educators will dispute that each student needs access to a quality education in order to compete in the larger society; however, the quality of instruction in every school in every school community is not the same. We *know* that some students receive a less rigorous education while other students are afforded and benefit from a higher quality education. Those other students afforded a higher-quality education are, as Orwell said in *Animal Farm,* "more equal than others." Educational attainment impacts individuals personally as well as influences the larger society. Just as the Data-Driven, Student-Centered Equity Framework is designed to show disparities in the school context, data describing larger social trends should also be used to describe the scope of the equity issues. The data describing disparities in educational equity may begin with a school community's examination of internal data, but the implications for life beyond K–12 are equally compelling. As a community of educators, we must understand that our work in the context of teaching and learning connects directly with students' abilities to become productive adults and their lifelong earning potential.

At this point in history, we are challenged to contend not only with the persistent achievement gap, but with the need to change the outcome of our work as educators. What students are expected to know and be able to do today is drastically different from the rote memorization required in the past. Educating each student well in the twenty-first century cannot be seen within the context of a broken student, people, or culture. We can negotiate the dilemma of difference by creating an educational equity agenda that uses rigorous standards for each student while still making necessary accommodations, if needed, for *some* students to be college and career ready.

The changing school population mirrors our changing society. Once stakeholders understand the scope of their schoolwide or districtwide equity challenge, they typically ask, "What are we going to do to meet the needs of our changing school populations?"

The equity framework allows leaders to guide the school community through assessing staff members' effectiveness in meeting student needs as the public school population continues to change rapidly. Given the influx of students from diverse backgrounds, instructional leaders must become skilled in communicating in accessible (and often multilingual) ways what each school's staff and students must do to achieve educational parity. They also must convey a sense of urgency because every day that we fail to meet students' learning needs is another day that we miss the opportunity to expand their learning opportunities. The PACE Framework explored in this book builds on the Data-Driven, Student-Centered Equity

Framework to show leaders how to address inequitable outcomes using the lens of staff beliefs and attitudes. Changes in these beliefs and attitudes regarding differences in socioeconomic status, language, race, ethnicity, and more are necessary to improve the achievement of students who now sit in and will continue to fill the desks of our schoolhouses.

DISCUSSION QUESTIONS AND ACTIVITIES

1. Consider the perspective that educators are people who bring their personal beliefs and values into the classroom. Would it be beneficial to assess the beliefs of the educators in your building or school district regarding the need to educate each student well? What mechanism would you use to collect this information? How do you think this information might inform your work within your instructional program?

2. Given your understanding of differences between and among student groups, identify any practices, protocols, and procedures that require students to conform to a single student group's norms or to preserve their differences. Examine your findings, and explain whether they serve to open educational access for students or whether they do the opposite.

3. Consider collecting data for one week to capture the unwritten, embedded beliefs held in your school or district. Keep a journal in which you record all comments you hear and observations you make (without names) relating to (a) a student's removal from a class or the school; (b) a student's ability (positive or negative); (c) specific student groups (for example, special education, free and reduced-price meal status, and/or English language learners); (d) students talking too much in class; (e) students not behaving in class; (f) college courses, trade courses, or job readiness courses; and (g) understanding educators' beliefs about educating each student well.

4. As your school or district implements the Common Core State Standards, how is your school or district addressing educators' beliefs associated with the importance of educating each student well? What plans have been made, if any, to help educators recognize underlying assumptions and hidden values about student success?

2 What Reform Has Taught Us

Now is a good time to ask whether we are on the right path to better schools. If not, we had better change fast if we want to be competitive in the world.

(Jennings, 2011)

Public education reform has been under way for the past fifty years, from President Lyndon Johnson's Elementary and Secondary Education Act to President Obama's Race to the Top programs. Federal policy has shaped state and local education priorities, most recently creating a focus on innovation; science, technology, engineering, and mathematics (STEM) education; and college and career readiness. To understand whether reforms have succeeded, we need to define the problems they were meant to address. What circumstances catalyzed the nation's need to reform public education? What statistics told us we needed corrective action in schooling America's children? Most important, what is the current status of issues we have attempted to address over the past sixty years? We examine these questions in this chapter.

School reform efforts have been minimally effective in improving outcomes for marginalized students. School reform, as realized over the past 50 years, has not resolved the equity issues that are plaguing us. Reform has yielded small gains and little organizational change. School transformation, which is what we argue for in this book, is discussed and implemented far less often. It is a longer-term proposition that aims to change organizations operationally and culturally. Transformation requires dismantling fundamental organizational practices that do not allow for equity.

Pursuing educational equity requires disrupting practices that marginalize, such as those that silence diverse perspectives and problematize children.

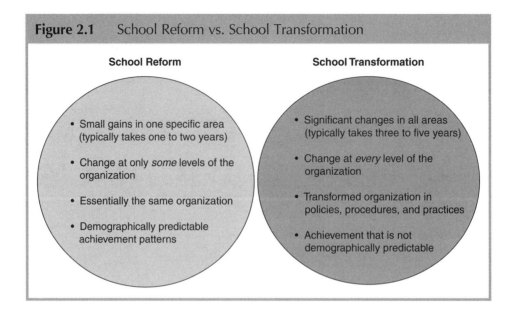

Figure 2.1   School Reform vs. School Transformation

School Reform

- Small gains in one specific area (typically takes one to two years)
- Change at only *some* levels of the organization
- Essentially the same organization
- Demographically predictable achievement patterns

School Transformation

- Significant changes in all areas (typically takes three to five years)
- Change at *every* level of the organization
- Transformed organization in policies, procedures, and practices
- Achievement that is not demographically predictable

In some places, the belief that the children are the problem is so pervasive that only outsiders can see it exists because it has become part of an unconscious organizational structure. Unless the structure is disrupted, the pattern of marginalizing children will continue. Transformation involves creating practices and procedures that are responsive to each student, not simply repackaging old ideas with a twist. Figure 2.1 summarizes the differences between school reform and school transformation.

School transformation involves changing school policies, procedures, and practices so that significant changes in outcome can be achieved. Leaders who want to pursue educational equity need first to identify the school practices that need to change in order to implement an equity agenda.

DISRUPTING DOMINANT CULTURAL PRACTICES: THE AWARENESS THAT MAKES EQUITY WORK POSSIBLE

Dominant cultural practices are powerful because they represent entrenched beliefs, making them difficult to combat and not readily identifiable as the principles driving the work. It is hard to change what is invisible. Consider, for example, how a dominant cultural practice marginalizes some students in a diverse population. Consider the idea that giving everyone the same materials, staffing, and so on will result in each student's achieving equitably high performance. If each student is to receive the same resources, how are individual students' unique needs and circumstances considered? Are they taken care of only after the majority's needs have been addressed? What resources are left then to support populations with potentially more intensive needs? Will students with specific needs be left with only supplemental support from grants, for example? Should support for vulnerable populations come only from supplemental resources?

By ensuring that everyone gets the same, educational equity is actually compromised. The failure to design reform efforts through an equity lens reflects a continuing pattern of marginalizing underserved students (see Figure 2.2). Public schools were not created to educate the student population that urban schools serve today, suggesting that we must do things that we haven't done and think in ways we have not thought previously.

Jayne Howard was considered an effective principal in a large high school serving more than 1,600 students, most of whom were African American and participants in the federal free and reduced-price meal program. Howard was first identified as an effective principal because she had managed to "turn around" the district's underperforming middle school—leading to the school's removal from the state's list of underperforming schools—before assuming the high school principalship. Howard said that, for her, reform meant firing teachers and creating a degree of fear. She never was able to decide or recommend what needed to happen at a school; she was told. In her district's middle and high schools, services, supports, and instruction for students were the last consideration. So much of her energy was dedicated to hiring staff, in fact, that she had minimal time to consider much else.

According to Fullan (2013, p. 20), in order to transform schools, "we need to shift our approach to the subjective experiences of students and engage them in new, meaningful and exciting ways." Howard reflected that neither school really "turned around." Although both schools were removed from the state's list of underperforming schools, achieving outcomes important to students and families had been a struggle.

Figure 2.2   Considering What Reform Has Meant in Your Experience

Answering the following questions will tell you a great deal about your priorities and practices, as well as how you have traditionally responded to equity challenges:

1. What has reform most often meant in your experience in education?
2. What was the level of awareness of staff, students, and the community about what the reform effort was and why it was necessary?
3. What role(s) have underperforming students served as reform efforts have been implemented?
4. How were reform efforts assessed?

For example, many of the students continued to be apathetic and disengaged in class, even as they prepared to graduate. Howard worried about their futures because many didn't plan to enter college or the workforce. Finally, as a result, she decided that the children needed to be central to any reform effort, so she created a teachers' academy to begin working with teachers to shift the school's paradigm.

Howard wanted teachers to become more instructionally responsive and to increase student engagement. She wanted staff to listen to student feedback, so she interviewed the school valedictorian from the prior year, who told the staff that he nearly flunked his freshman year of college. This was the context teachers needed, Howard said. She set up team meetings throughout the year with content teachers; those meetings were facilitated by the content area chairperson and a student leader, and the meetings focused on student work samples. By the end of the school year, fewer students had been suspended from school, a leadership culture was developing among students, and teachers had a broader array of options to employ during instruction. Howard shaped her school's work to meet student needs.

For leaders, the driving force behind decisions should be how to shape actions to benefit *each* student. As you reflect on Howard's experience, consider the driving force for the change process in your building or district. Is it a mandate? Is it a compliance requirement? Although these are typical pressures to which school leaders must respond, this chapter examines why actions that emerge as responses to mandates and compliance requirements are not sufficient to advance an equity agenda. We encourage you to examine your own experience as we explore what reform has taught us.

WHAT LED US TO THE REFORM CONVERSATION?

In 1964, President Johnson addressed Congress and suggested that the Economic Opportunity Act was an opportunity to give "underprivileged young Americans the opportunity to develop skills, continue education, and find useful work" (Johnson, 1964). Johnson's "War on Poverty" was responsible for creating Head Start, an early education intervention, and the Title I program, the largest federal government contribution to public education. Both programs continue today. Johnson thought the nation could conquer poverty, provide equitable education, and expand opportunities to work, all of which would benefit families and society at large. He believed America would be stronger when the underserved were brought from the periphery into the mainstream. The education community responded with the first wave of contemporary reform—addressing the needs of economically disadvantaged students.

Wave 1: Addressing Educational Equity for Economically Disadvantaged Students

Title I funding continues to influence public education as federal money flows into schools to enhance the academic achievement of economically disadvantaged students, most often in reading and math. Historically, reading and math support was delivered through a "pull-out" model. A Title I resource teacher would come to the general education class, remove the Title I students, provide small-group instruction, and then return those students to the general education class.

Students removed from the general education setting were denied access to the core curriculum for which they were also held responsible. The interventions often were not coordinated with the pacing of the curriculum so that students were challenged to connect skills taught in isolation with the larger concepts that the skills were intended to support. It was like arriving late at a movie and trying to fill in the earlier scenes based on the current conversation—a difficult task for already-struggling students.

Although the achievement gap between white and non-white (African American and Hispanic) students has narrowed since 1964, the gap has not closed. A prominent gap remains, and in terms of socioeconomic indicators, the gap has widened since the first wave of reform to the present (National Assessment of Educational Progress, 2012). More meaningful is the finding that, among black and brown families, nearly one-third currently live in poverty (U.S. Census, 2010). Perhaps more meaningful is the finding that among black families, nearly one-third currently live in poverty and just over 25 percent of brown families live in poverty as well (DeNavas-Walt, Proctor, & Smith, 2013). If social and economic mobility are outcomes that result from better educational preparation, and test data are a significant means for describing educational preparation, then poverty statistics suggest that there is much work left to be done.

Wave 1 Critical Learning

Our reform efforts have taught us that low-level instruction has a crippling effect on attempts to mitigate predictable patterns of low educational attainment.

Lessons From Wave 1 Reforms

We sometimes question whether the investment in public education has offered an acceptable yield. Less often do we analyze how we have used the investment itself. The use of intervention or remediation to address student underperformance has proven to be based on faulty logic, yet that logic is often applied to schools serving large numbers of black, brown, and poor students. This type of reform-minded thinking satiates the general public for the moment because, done well, it can provide quick, observable increases in achievement data. However, students who need academic acceleration, who need to make more than one year's growth during one year of instruction, need richer and meaningful exposure to a robust teaching and learning experience. Even when we make gains in closing achievement gaps, that achievement should happen in tandem with *real* outcomes in learners' lives. If students are better prepared by being better educated, this should also mean they are better prepared to manage life beyond that which can be measured by standardized assessments. If the only measure of better preparation is higher test scores (with no other real-life correlates), then the question that remains is: What did we really reform?

Testing Accountability and Authentic Student Learning

Student assessment and accountability for performance are not going away. Standardized assessment data should be balanced with other data that tell us about students' access to learning opportunities. Data are helpful only when they offer insights into *why* as well as *what.* Educators need quality information that describes students' access to learning opportunities more than they need information about what students have learned. Leaders pursuing educational equity have a dual role. Because of increasing accountability, transparency, and reporting requirements, leaders need assessments that help the school community understand student challenges and successes. But they also need to make clear that the vision driving the school goes beyond student achievement on tests. Increasing test scores is powerful only if the tests indicate increased student learning, yet improved test scores don't necessarily mean student learning has improved.

If activities required of students are of low cognitive demand and student engagement is minimal, then the challenge is enhancing teaching and learning practice, not increasing test scores. Data describing stubborn, persistent gaps in achievement often lead us to infer that the problem is *certain* children and not access to quality instruction. Low-level instruction is a counterproductive practice that is more likely to be found in schools with students from diverse backgrounds (Boykin & Noguera, 2011; Delpit, 2012). If we believe that school is connected to preparation for life after K–12, then data that indicate no substantive difference in college enrollment rates (or participation in remedial college coursework), graduation rates, and/or income levels should prompt us to ask, "What did we actually reform?"

Thinking Forward to Apply Lessons Learned

As you consider your vision of equity, how will you assess access to quality instruction? The first wave of education reform taught us that we cannot transform outcomes without transforming input. Access to quality daily instruction is the input that can make a huge difference in the outcomes. *More* (more reading time, more math time, more time in summer school, etc.) doesn't equate to the quality learning that underperforming students need. Research shows that quality instruction has six times the impact of poor instruction (Haycock, 2005). Quality instruction minimizes the use of intervention or remediation and the time a student spends in intervention.

To move toward equity, leaders need to ensure that assessments of quality instruction are linked to demonstrations of students' learning. We must move away from the old model that suggests that good instruction can be observed as little more than a series of activities itemized on a checklist. The pursuit of educational equity challenges leaders to consider quality instruction through a prism that considers the cultural, transactional nature of teaching and learning. In a transformed school, assessments are used judiciously, and there are times when itemized checklists are not meaningful or useful at all. Figure 2.3 outlines key questions to help leaders think about restructuring a school's instructional program.

Wave 1 Lessons

1. Students need access to a robust, relevant core curricular program;
2. Students in need of acceleration need more exposure and more access to meaningful learning opportunities; and
3. Quality instruction should be defined by outcomes associated with quality student performance.

┌───┐
| **Figure 2.3**   Questions for Reflection |
├───┤

1. What is your primary philosophy for accelerating student achievement? What is the evidence of this?
2. How are services being delivered to underperforming students (during the day, before or after school, through pull-out sessions, etc.)? Does this service model have a positive impact on students, as you assess multiple data points?
3. Are your general education teachers (not just specialists) equipped with the skills and knowledge required to meet your students' acceleration needs? What evidence are you using to understand your teachers' abilities to accelerate learning?
4. Have you conceptualized the acceleration needs of your students as central or peripheral to the overall work of the school? What is the evidence for your assertion?

└───┘

Wave 2: A Nation at Risk: Standards-Based Reform

In 1983, the National Commission on Excellence in Education released the report *A Nation at Risk: The Imperative for Educational Reform*. The commission was created in response to then–secretary of education T. H. Bell's concern about the "widespread public perception that something [was] seriously remiss in our educational system" (National Commission on Excellence in Education, 1983, p. 7). Despite the twenty years of education reform that the Elementary and Secondary Education Act had begun, the public still perceived that something was not quite right in public education. *A Nation at Risk* opened with the assertion that mediocrity was eroding our future. The authors maintained that the evidence of this erosion was that others (foreign nations) were surpassing U.S. educational attainments. With a sense of urgency related to the potential loss of global hegemony, the commission offered the following preamble for readers' consideration (National Commission on Excellence in Education, 1983):

> All, regardless of race or class or economic status, are entitled to a fair chance and to the tools for developing their individual powers of mind and spirit to the utmost. This promise means that all children by virtue of their own efforts, competently guided, can hope to attain the mature and informed judgment needed to secure gainful employment, and to manage their own lives, thereby serving not only their interests but also the progress of society itself.

As you reflect on these ideas, clear themes emerge. Issues of fairness, equality, as well as students' accountability are pronounced. It followed that the action most critical was leveling of the educational playing field to provide equal education, the theme that we use to define the second wave of reform—the standards-based movement. The premise of standards-based reform is that if a state requires a given body of content to be mastered by all students, as assessed by a common testing instrument, then school districts will create systems of support that create equal opportunity for all students to be successful. How often have you seen the image in Figure 2.4?

The amount of attention paid to ensuring that the curriculum and resources are aligned to state standards has consumed a good deal of our energy since the release of *A Nation at Risk.* Curriculum offices, school leadership, and teachers not only want to know that materials are aligned to the state's standards; they also want to ensure that materials are formatted similarly to the state test. These concerns are completely understandable and appropriate responses to standards-based reform. This is because the unstated hypothesis of standards-based reform is that alignment (among the written, assessed, and taught curriculum) is both the problem and the solution to challenges in meeting the needs of each student.

Unpacking the Lessons From Wave 2 of Education Reform

What have been the consequences of the standards-based reform movement's efforts to align the written, taught, and assessed curriculum? The most observable consequence has been implementation and assessment of the written curriculum. Scripted curricula have been popular products in this wave of reform, in which teachers are handed lesson plans that virtually dictate what they say to the class. The guiding thought is that if students are exposed to the same standards, then the issue of equal access to the same learning requirements is solved. An unintended consequence is that rich discussion of instructional practices, and by extension student engagement, has been underemphasized.

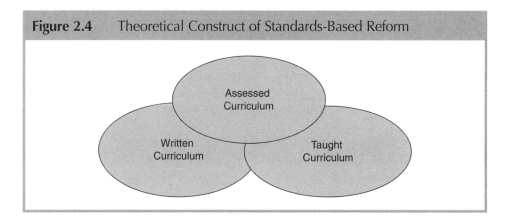

Figure 2.4 Theoretical Construct of Standards-Based Reform

Teachers serving underperforming students wrestle with having enough time to *cover the curriculum*. They have to narrow the curriculum to cover a given amount of content in a given period of time to meet state assessment requirements. This is certainly not a desirable reform outcome. Scripted or time-specific curricula allow school administrators and central office personnel to know which teachers are not covering the curriculum. Precise timelines tell school leaders where in the curriculum teachers should be (down to the day and class period) to prepare for the benchmark assessment.

What Do Data Show About the Effectiveness of Reform?

National Assessment of Educational Progress (NAEP) data from 1973 to 2008 show little progress in accelerating each student's performance and little progress in closing gaps in achievement (NAEP, 2012). Gaps that can be measured by using socioeconomic status show similar patterns of disparity in students' performance (NAEP, 2012).

Figure 2.5 describes a transformative model for reforming the schooling process that addresses three critical areas overlooked by traditional models. The focal points are who is teaching, who the learners are, and how skills and concepts are taught. To improve outcomes for each student, these areas deserve as much consideration as aligning the written, taught, and assessed curriculum.

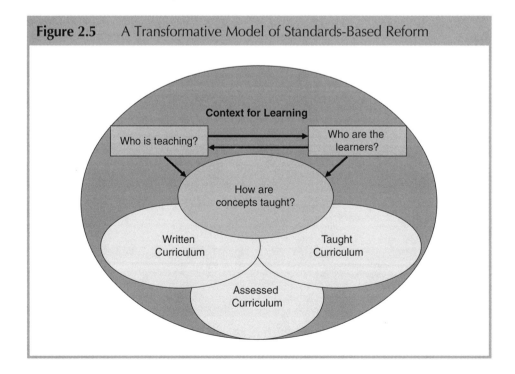

Figure 2.5   A Transformative Model of Standards-Based Reform

Furthermore, and of critical importance, in a transformative model, the question of how concepts are best taught and learned is actively considered. A transformative model recognizes that teaching is influenced directly by the instructor's knowledge of the student as learner.

Teaching to Make Learning Transactions

Teaching is not unidirectional. Transactions from teacher to student, from student to teacher, and from student to student all occur in a rich learning environment. Student learning is a function of the person providing the instruction. We have sought to answer the question, Who is teaching the students? by creating certification requirements and labels like "highly qualified." The real answer to the question, Who is teaching the students? goes beyond what a teacher knows (in terms of content knowledge). Descriptions of teacher competency in twenty-first-century teaching and learning should include the teacher's knowledge and capacity to use *soft* skills effectively. Soft skills, such as the ability to build relationships, intercultural competency, the ability to use technology intuitively to enhance learning, and the ability to support innovative inquiry meaningfully, are critical considerations as we think about who is teaching students.

The public conversation about preparing twenty-first-century learners often fails to outline the scope of the challenge facing public education. In many instances, we are asking teachers who were trained to provide twentieth-century instruction to prepare twenty-first-century learners. The same can be said of leaders. The shifts that have made our world different from the twentieth century to the twenty-first century are not simple. The shift from an industrial to a knowledge-based economy is not a small matter. Furthermore, the shift in student demographics has created tension in terms of teachers' capacities to address the more diverse cultural frameworks in which learning occurs. Students' development of soft skills like communication, teamwork, critical thinking, and problem solving is yet another significant reality in educator accountability as we consider skills that students need to graduate high school ready for life.

Teachers who understand the transactional nature of teaching and learning are more likely to understand the need to adjust their daily (in some instances, moment-to-moment) practices when students don't learn. Education leaders create a climate in which adjustment and adaptive instruction are common practices. In equity work, the ability to make adjustments and adaptations skillfully is a critical capacity when the expectation is that teaching and learning are coupled. Teachers working in an environment where this is the standard creatively adjust even the curriculum to students' learning needs. They are primed to prepare students for a world in which what we know is only as valuable as what we can do with that knowledge. This is what teachers focused on equitable outcomes know and do; leaders focused on equity create these standards as cultural norms.

When the focus is not on equity as assessed by outcomes, teaching and learning is unidirectional—the teacher teaches; the student learns. The older the students, the more likely it is that teachers expect that they learn distilled information. Teachers who see themselves as distillers of information move through the curriculum following strict timelines. Covering the curriculum, rather than students' learning, drives instruction. Leaders not dialed into equity may not recognize that a teacher who shows this compliance-driven instructional behavior is a staff member who needs assistance. Some of these teachers, in fact, may have been highlighted as examples of what can be accomplished. Without delving into data about student performance and examining how different groups of students are achieving, it is impossible to know how well that instructor is meeting students' needs.

Focusing only on what is to be taught has led to the unintended consequence of failing to look at teachers' capacities. A myopic focus on teacher certification has diverted attention from developing teachers' abilities to implement instructional strategies effectively (Stigler & Hiebert, 1999).

Traditional standards-based reform does not respond directly to evidence provided by unsuccessful students that perhaps we need to extend our model beyond alignment among the written, taught, and assessed curriculum. Although credentials partly describe teacher skills, the methods that teachers are able to use with students are the indicators of their effectiveness. Teachers' abilities to attend to student engagement and interest is critical for deep and meaningful learning. Additionally, we need students to be active partners in the teaching and learning transaction. As such, any model for reform that fails to contend with the challenge of actively engaging an increasingly diverse learning population is missing a significant aspect of the complexity of modern teaching and learning.

Wave 2 Lessons

1. Curriculum developed to support standards must be relevant to students.
2. Effective instructional practice yields evidence that the learning needs of each student are being met.
3. Knowing the student as a learner is critical as teachers make decisions about effective instructional practices.
4. Affective domain considerations are not subordinate to cognitive domain considerations.

The Problem of Color Blindness

To be more responsive in expanding and extending students' learning opportunities, we must know them and consider who they are as learners. Wave 2 of education reform advanced the notion that *color blindness* was an appropriate equality strategy. Although the idea of color blindness is typically associated with race, the idea includes a general sense that, to be fair, one must treat all students the same. The strategy eases educators' discomfort when they feel challenged by the differences posed by students. We maintain that it is the silence around the differences rather than the differences themselves that make responding difficult. Furthermore, and just as important, managing the change in teacher praxis that should happen with increased knowledge of the learner is another essential element that has been absent in this wave of reform. Knowledge of students' cultural frameworks is critical for making teaching and learning rich and relevant when the only other perspectives are those of the teacher and the curriculum. If deep and meaningful learning is a consequence of the learner's active engagement, then the question of who our students are and what they want and need to be engaged is essential. Think about this idea as you consider the experience of Adrianna Ramirez.

Adrianna Ramirez was principal of an alternative high school of about 200 largely African American and Hispanic economically challenged students. She had made positive changes in her four years of leadership that had improved the safety and overall climate of the school community, but she was frustrated as she began to take stock of other data describing the school's progress. Ramirez understood that the improvements she could count paled in comparison to data that painted the picture of quality of life after high school. The majority of students had grade point averages below 2.0 on a 4.0 scale.

Among students taking the SAT (assuming that these students were the best prepared), the average score was just over 1100 out of a possible 2400. Also, although participation in Advanced Placement (AP) courses had increased, few of those students received passing scores on the AP exams. Ramirez didn't want alternative high school to mean holding a place until graduation. She had a vision that the school would provide a rich experience for students' unique needs. As she prepared to move into another school year, she considered conversations she had had with a few of the young men who were graduating. It was clear the students did not believe anyone had high expectations for them. It wasn't that the young men believed people had low expectations of them; they simply believed people had no expectations of them.

According to the young men she spoke with, they knew that no one believed in them because teachers constantly let them off the hook.

Teachers did not hold them accountable. If teachers had asked or cared, the young men said, they might have tried harder. They told stories of struggles they were managing but did not talk about at school as the reasons for their misbehavior. They said they felt there were no adults they could trust with whom they could share their problems.

Ramirez was moved by what the students shared, so much so that she decided that all staff would be required to address the affective domain in teaching and learning. She believed that small acts could make big differences for children. Before she moved forward with this training for teachers, she wanted a better picture of the schoolwide perception of what she called the "care factor." She had all students take a perceptual survey, and the data were telling. Students reported that they did not know whether teachers cared about them, and they didn't like or care about the teachers. Students said they felt disengaged, and they said the material they were learning had no relevance to the real world. Interestingly, students believed they were doing their "best work."

As Ramirez conferred with staff to analyze the meaning of these data, she posed one powerful question: "How can we turn this around if our students feel disengaged while at the same time feel they are giving their best effort?" Then she asked, "How can we convey to them that we care and are invested in their success? Do you see how this disconnect must be addressed if we are ever to give students real access to a meaningful educational experience?" For Ramirez, changing the perception climate was the first step in addressing the academic concerns.

Through Ramirez's experiences, we see how day-to-day realities limit one's ability to respond to the subtleties that often depress student performance when standards-based reform is implemented. Concentrating on standards, instruction, and assessment, though important, cannot break through the barriers of disenfranchisement. Active engagement is a minimum requirement for doing one's best. Stressing standards with passive learners will only expand underperformance rather than mitigating or eliminating it. Cultural mismatch or incongruence affects students of diverse backgrounds (Ogbu,1992). The striking demographic differences between the educational community (racially and socioeconomically) and the growing diverse student population creates conditions that are ripe for cultural incongruence. If students are to achieve at their highest potential, adults facilitating their learning cannot just skip past the existence of a belief system that would never allow high achievement to be possible. Finally, research is beginning to show promise that social-psychological interventions can be used to build relationships and address students' thoughts and beliefs (mindset) that may be impeding their success (Dweck, 2006; Yeager & Walton, 2011).

Educators who work to achieve equity consider student knowledge, strive to engage students in learning, and develop student mindsets that foster persistence (see Figure 2.6). Lessons learned from Wave 2 of contemporary education reform have shown us that efforts focused only on aligning curriculum, assessment, and instruction do not eliminate achievement gaps.

To transform schooling to serve each student, educators must account for the social, cultural, and emotional learning context to create a fuller platform for student engagement. Curriculum guides and teacher preparation courses don't include all the domains essential to learning. It is up to educators to develop and expand their understanding of quality instruction.

Wave 3: Common Core State Standards

The Common Core State Standards extend traditional standards-based reform because they increase accountability in two significant ways. First, they are a set of national standards that in theory will allow for state-to-state comparisons. Because states did not have common standards, arguments ensued about the fairness of using the NAEP for comparisons. Second, according to the standards, students should be certifiable as college or workforce ready upon graduation (Conley, 2011).

Figure 2.6   Questions for Consideration

As you consider the impact of the second wave of education reform, reflect on these questions:

1. How have you assessed the responsiveness of your core curriculum to the needs of your diverse populations? How do you know the curriculum is interesting and engaging to each learner?
2. Which instructional methods currently in use in your school or district are optimal for learning for your students?
3. What evidence do you have that these methods are optimal for every learner?
4. Are you aware of the presence or absence of significant student-centric, academically related cognitive dispositions that characterize your student population (for example, internal versus external locus of control, growth versus fixed mindset, avoidance behaviors, self-advocacy, self-regulation)?
5. Have you provided your staff with training and support to help them understand and respond to the development of academically related cognitive dispositions in the teaching and learning process?
6. How have you provided leadership that holds staff accountable for responding to these factors?

"A student who is ready for college and career can qualify for and succeed in entry-level, credit-bearing college courses leading to a baccalaureate or certificate, or career pathway-oriented training programs without the need for remedial or developmental coursework" (Conley, 2012, p. 1). Yet according to Complete College America (2012), approximately 67 percent of African American students entering two-year colleges (39 percent entering four-year), 58 percent of Hispanic students entering two-year colleges (20 percent entering four-year), and 64 percent of low-income students entering two-year college (31 percent entering four-year) enroll needing remediation. Responding to these data in the K–12 pipeline will require leaders to think critically about students' access to and success in rigorous course offerings. In terms of students' being prepared for the workforce immediately upon graduation, 2014 unemployment statistics showed that 19.3 percent of young people could not find work (FRED Economic Research, 2014). This is almost three times the overall national unemployment rate of 6.7 percent (U.S. Bureau of Labor Statistics, 2014). If we are to prepare every student to meet twenty-first-century demands, we need to begin by taking stock of what we have learned and think differently about how we get students where they need to go. The challenge we face at this moment is how to increase standards for each student while forthrightly addressing the gaps that exist in our respective schools and districts.

Accountability for schools and school districts in ensuring that students can successfully engage in life after K–12 is uncharted territory in public education. Data alone should force the educational community to address the question of relevance: Is education relevant to students, society, business, national security, and expectations for active citizenship? Also, what are the metrics by which these ideas will be assessed? We are forming the working definition of college-ready students, but how far will the definition of workforce readiness expand? School leaders need to contend with these issues as society reevaluates the role of education in society.

It is clear that the drumbeat of increasing accountability expectations among stakeholders outside of the educational community is a reality. We can begin by both facing and addressing the reality that past solutions are insufficient to address current challenges in public education. Our contemporary history of school reform shows us that. The most politically charged element of the current reform is increased attention to global competition. Technology, economies of scale, inexpensive labor, and increased access to education for disenfranchised groups have created a global marketplace. It is our responsibility to provide our marginalized students with the education they need in order to participate as adults in dynamic growth fields such as science, technology, engineering, and mathematics.

According to the Common Core State Standards website (Council of Chief State School Officers & National Governors Association, 2012), the standards do NOT define the following:

- How teachers should teach
- All that can or should be taught
- The nature of advanced work beyond the core
- The interventions needed for students well below grade level
- The full range of support for English language learners and students with special needs
- Everything needed to be college and career ready

No initiative can respond to every contingency. Students' learning and emotional support needs can vary between two communities separated by only a few city blocks or a few miles of rural roads. However, the most substantive challenges faced by public school systems and schools across this country are the items the authors of the Common Core State Standards have chosen not to address.

From Reform to Transformation

Despite past efforts at reform, demographically predictable underperformance is still evident in schools and districts across the country. NAEP achievement has improved in some areas, but gaps have not closed or been eliminated in any of the areas that existed before these reforms were undertaken (NAEP, 2012). Alarmingly, gaps based on economic variables have widened in recent years. Public education is not serving as the engine of social mobility that our society needs. Robust curricula, fair and adequate resources, and appropriate use of assessment measures are needed educational tools, but collectively they still will not lead to educational equity. Those committed to the pursuit of educational equity should use the evidence of the insufficiency of past reforms to engage in transformation. Transformation, which we examine in the remaining chapters in the book, must be realized through the lessons from our past. As we begin to conceptualize what it means to pursue educational equity through the lens of our underserved populations, we must examine policies, practices, and procedures. When the lived experiences of our diverse students differ in ways that challenge daily practice, the equity imperative requires that we adapt. In essence, the equity imperative implores us to craft our practice through the learning needs of those who are underserved by the status quo. This is how we characterize the heart of transformation: the consent to have policies, procedures, and practices subject to outcomes based on equitable access to quality instruction.

When demographically predictable achievement shows up as a trend, leaders take action to interrupt behaviors that perpetuate its occurrence.

Clearly our methods warrant examination since we have not met our reform goal of achieving educational equity. Research on mindset, the impact of stress on learning, technology to increase collaborative opportunities, and more suggest a need to expand thinking and practices to ensure access to quality instruction for each student. The transition to Common Core State Standards presents another opportunity for us to attempt to address the learning needs of each student. We can take this moment to reconsider what is necessary, given that what we have done in the past is not sufficient. As you continue to read and reflect on the process and strategies we recommend in the upcoming chapters, we encourage you resist the tendency to implement the latest reform that doesn't substantively challenge past practice. We encourage you to commit to transformation to the pursuit of educational equity.

CONCLUSION

Principals and district leaders are publicly accountable for every student group entering the schoolhouse doors. Innovative, outside-the-box, and throw-away-the-box thinking shows what's possible in public education. School leaders can transform schooling if they have a vision for high achievement outcomes for each student and are armed with a mechanism to guide and manage education innovation to ensure execution of that vision. We can map achievement gaps all along the public school continuum, and these gaps continue to occur after more than fifty years of school reform. Transforming our practices begins by taking this approach.

The education reforms that we have implemented, while successful in some ways, will not get us to the goal of educational equity. Perhaps even more sobering is the fact that our democratic, resourceful country has such stark social and economic disparities compared with other nations that have fewer resources. These realities tell us that we have work to do. To serve a diverse student population, we must begin to negotiate the school transformation process.

Today, we face the challenge of preparing each student for the demands of college or the workforce. This challenge demands that we think critically about what it means to engage students on a daily basis in a manner that prepares them for the larger society. These decisions need to be made with the context of our students at the fore—*each* of our students. Using the prism of transformation toward equity as a frame, leaders can move their campuses and districts forward. Transformation is a substantively different proposition than reform or turnaround. The complexity of what needs to occur in daily practice to ensure that each student has access to quality instruction and academic engagement requires a willingness to change course. We have to be willing to have discussions we have never had and to try materials we have never considered. When we find what meets our underserved students' needs, we must institutionalize it as school or district practice. School processes today remain centered around a middle-class, Eurocentric, industrial model of preparation. Yet today's public school students can largely be characterized as economically and culturally diverse. The economy and the workforce have transitioned from an industrial age to a digital, information age. Transformed practices are needed to respond to these realities.

Addressing the dilemmas of difference and the imperative to change to meet the needs of each learner characterize the current moment in public education. We must examine and embrace school transformation. Efforts we undertake should position us to respond to gaps that, left unattended, will only widen. Use Part II of this book and the discussion questions below to reflect on how you will realize the transformation toward equity needed in your school or district.

DISCUSSION QUESTIONS AND ACTIVITIES

1. Have you engaged staff in an analysis of your school's or district's reforms, identifying any disparity in outcomes that remains?

2. Do staff members understand the difference between reform and transformation?

3. Do educators in your school or district understand the need to transform their practices?

4. To what degree does your school or district engage in practices associated with the lessons learned from problems with school reform?

5. As you implement the Common Core State Standards, how do you see classroom instruction changing? How is it staying the same?

6. What evidence do you have that teachers are regularly offering each student access to experiences that will put them on track for college and careers?

7. Do teachers believe that the shifts that are occurring in your school or district are primarily an issue of changing curriculum? If yes, how do you plan to broaden your staff's vision of all that must change to realize the goal of better-prepared students?

8. How are you vetting practices and procedures through a lens that examines equity?

3

The PACE Framework for Equity

Merging Job-Embedded Equity Learning Cycles With Ongoing Data Analysis

It is always easier to blame the victims. Often when we hear this statement, we are referring to students; however, the same can be said of teachers.

—Nashae Bennett, elementary school principal, January 19, 2014

The phone rang at Esther Jenkins's house one summer evening about 8:30 p.m. It was her deputy superintendent, asking her to accept reassignment to a principalship at one of the district's twelve high schools and pressing her to make a decision immediately. Caught off guard and with no time to research the position, Jenkins was flattered by the faith the deputy superintendent expressed in her abilities and agreed to take the post. She didn't know if she'd have another opportunity if she passed on this one. When she arrived at the school a week later, she learned that she would be the fifth principal assigned to the school within the past seven years. One of the four assistant principals was out on medical leave, and eight of her sixty teaching positions were vacant. Then she found that all eight vacancies were in the English as a Second Language (ESL) department. Since 86 percent of the student population participated in the ESL program, Jenkins was more than a little concerned. She had little previous training with the ESL curricula or evidence-based teaching strategies linked to increasing achievement for English language learners.

Next, she reviewed students' graduation rates, performance on state assessments, and college enrollment rates. As she reviewed the accountability data, she learned that less than 60 percent of students graduated the prior year, 40 percent of students met standards on the state assessments on their first assessment attempt, and only 15 percent of graduates enrolled immediately in a two- or four-year postsecondary program. Jenkins called her supervisor to share her concerns. In addition to offering support, her supervisor told Jenkins to use her innate leadership skills, to schedule an immediate meeting with the district's ESL director, and to create an entry plan and a one-year plan focused on the work within her control. Jenkins hung up feeling more encouraged.

Principals frequently are placed in assignments without full knowledge of the context or the skill set needed for them to increase student achievement. Too often they have no clue about the achievement gaps that exist at their new schools. The reality of the challenges that they and their schools face, for some principals in some school districts, likely contributes to the high turnover rates among principals. The inability to retain principals, combined with the average two- to three-year tenures of superintendents, has raised the question of whether public schools can establish and maintain effective structures to produce positive student outcomes for all. Some observers maintain that alternatives to public education can be more effective in helping students achieve academic success (Cuban & Tyack, 1995; Elmore, 1997; Gill, Timpane, Ross, & Brewer, 2001). We believe public schools *can* be highly successful for each student *if* leaders are thoughtful, organized, and equipped with a systematic process for staying focused on teaching each student.

The PACE Framework for Equity is a tool that helps principals eliminate barriers associated with student underperformance. It combines findings about quality teaching and learning practices, culturally responsive instruction, data analysis, protocols for data meetings, assessment, and job-embedded professional development with practical implementation. The educational equity framework outlined in Chapter 1 is implicit within the PACE Framework. The PACE Framework helps school leaders to normalize daily quality instruction for *each* student—a student's race, culture, religion, disability, socioeconomic status, educational gaps, primary language, home environment, parent's education, and school readiness are key considerations to determine what is needed in the school community to promote quality daily instruction.

PACE is transformational, involving drastic and permanent changes to programs, structures, and processes that contribute to student underperformance. PACE does not simply suggest more of the same. Research supporting elements of the PACE Framework is plentiful (Bambrick-Santoyo, 2010; Bernhardt, 2004; Blythe, Allen, & Powell, 1999; DuFour, Eaker,

Karthanek, & DuFour, 2004; Ellis, 2001; Fullan, 1999, 2001, 2008; Guskey, 2000; Johnson, 2002; Kelley & Shaw, 2009; Marzano, 2003; Marzano & Heflebower, 2001; Marzano & Pickering, 2010; Scheurich & Skrla, 2003; Wellman & Lipton, 2004). The framework is a fluid, cyclical process framed by four essential actions (see Figure 3.1):

1. P—principal's instructional vision for equity

2. A—assessment of the teaching and learning dynamic

3. C—collaborative, job-embedded equity learning cycles (Equity learning cycles are instructional rounds that include a protocol designed intentionally to examine equity and access considerations within the school community.)

4. E—evaluation of the equity learning cycles, transfer of equity learning cycles to change of practice, refinement and continuation of the framework

The four essential actions frame the analysis, evaluation, and examination of data from the equity framework.

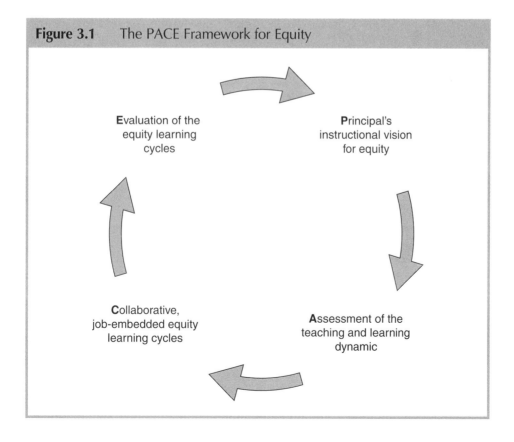

Figure 3.1   The PACE Framework for Equity

Evaluation of the equity learning cycles

Principal's instructional vision for equity

Collaborative, job-embedded equity learning cycles

Assessment of the teaching and learning dynamic

CREATE AN INSTRUCTIONAL VISION FOR THE TEACHING AND LEARNING DYNAMIC

Principals—not federal legislation, state laws, or local reform efforts— are the true agents of change to ensure that each student has access to a quality instructional program every day (Boykin & Noguera, 2011). Effective principals possess a unique skill set and are willing to live in the question: What can we refine or do differently to ensure that each student is college or work ready upon high school graduation? To realize the true power of the PACE Framework, consider the belief statements in Figure 3.2. The framework challenges you to reexamine your work and actions in order to confront the achievement gap and create conditions for each student to be engaged in high-quality instruction in every classroom every day.

Principals often unconsciously make excuses for disparate student outcomes. To make the unconscious conscious, principals outline an instructional vision to guide the teaching and learning dynamic with an expressed focus on equity. The *teaching and learning dynamic* is a complex interaction that includes (a) who is teaching; (b) who the learners are; and (c) what concepts are being taught (the convergence of the written, taught, and assessed). These components interact as learners work toward instructional goals to incorporate new knowledge, behaviors, and skills that complement and enhance their experiences. The teaching and learning dynamic includes teachers' ability to engage diverse learners and relate to them; teachers' ability to communicate content to those learners; students' ability to connect new learning to prior knowledge and construct new meaning from additional information; and the environment that engages and stimulates the learning process (Perelman, 1992; Rosenshine, 1995).

Figure 3.2   Assertions Essential to the PACE Framework

1. I know that school transformation must occur from within the school, not from outside it.
2. I know that each student can be successful and can meet local, state, and federal standards.
3. I know that teachers want to be successful and are well intentioned; however, they are not, in many instances, equipped with the technical skills needed to educate *each* student well.
4. I know that school-based and district-level leaders often expect teachers to implement curricula, interventions, instructional strategies, and technology without providing teachers with the requisite professional development.
5. I know that we must negotiate fiscal and human resources for schools to contend creatively and innovatively with the goal of educating each student well.

Principals need a thoughtful, comprehensive, and *shared* instructional vision for teaching and learning that focuses deliberately on equity. The school's shared vision is the springboard to an instructional vision. However, even if a school leader is assigned to a school that doesn't have a vision or mission, he or she should not wait until the school community drafts vision and mission statements before creating an equity-focused instructional vision.

Allen Lowe, for example, was assigned to a school without a school vision, mission, or improvement plan. He decided to work on creating an instructional vision while a planning team collaborated on creating a school vision. The team collected data (informal and formal observation data; student work; student cumulative folders; teacher personnel folders; meeting notes; state assessments; local assessments; and interviews with selected staff, students, parents/guardians, and community members). Then, the team convened a committee of representatives from stakeholder groups (teachers, students, parents/guardians, and community members). In four meetings, the committee analyzed the data and began drafting a school vision. They introduced the school vision to the entire school community for a vote. It was approved with a few minor amendments. To align all work done in the school, the school vision committee reviewed school traditions, rituals, and processes to ensure that they could and would be included in the school vision. The principal's process was clear and succinct, and it promoted collaboration and transparency. Lowe introduced his instructional vision that same week to focus his work as the school's instructional leader.

Nanus (1992) offers guidance in creating a shared, collaborative, and goal-oriented school vision. A collaborative school vision is a holistic snapshot from the vantage point of stakeholders—teachers, parents/guardians, administrators, students, and community members. Figure 3.3 will help principals to distinguish between a school vision and an instructional vision.

Components of a Principal's Instructional Vision

The principal's instructional vision is the catalyst for PACE. The instructional vision outlines expectations for all stakeholders (students, teachers, administrators, support staff, and parents/guardians) and ensures that stakeholders understand the focus of student learning and how it will be demonstrated for all using an equity perspective. The principal's instructional vision should be shared with critical stakeholder groups as a living and evolving extension of the school's vision. While the instructional vision keeps the school leader focused and accountable, teachers use the instructional vision to transform their behavior, but this realization is a process (Sergiovanni, 1990).

Figure 3.3 Distinguishing the School Vision From the Equity-Focused Instructional Vision

School Vision	Equity-Focused Instructional Vision
• Focuses on all aspects of the school community • Outlines what the school aspires to do for each student, which includes commentary about the learning environment, contributions to the larger school community, and extracurricular activities • Describes general characteristics of all stakeholders: students, teachers, administrators, support staff, and parents/guardians • Is based on collaboration with all stakeholders	• Focuses exclusively on the teaching and learning dynamic • Outlines specifically what administrators, teachers, support staff, and students are expected to do daily • Describes what strategies will be used to support excellence in each class for each student • Delineates what metrics of success will be used to assess whether or not stakeholders' behaviors are translating into increased achievement for each student group

As the school community engages in the PACE Framework, the principal revisits the instructional vision to refine it, if needed, based on lessons learned through implementing PACE.

An accessible equity-focused instructional vision describes ideal teacher, student, and parent/guardian behaviors, as well as the conditions for an optimal learning environment. It outlines these behaviors through the three prongs of the equity framework and defines the metrics of success. To provide a preferred learning environment, principals create an instructional vision supported by the belief that a master schedule provides teachers with (a) time-on-task opportunities to present rigorous, authentic, grade-level content and (b) time-on-task opportunities to address gaps in students' skills. Effective teaching and learning in every classroom is the critical component of contending with adverse achievement trend data, but optimal learning conditions are a basic requirement as well. Principals should create a master schedule that gives teachers enough time for flexible grouping and extended learning time while ensuring that students in self-contained special education classes can be included in general education classes, when appropriate.

When possible, the equity-focused instructional vision should emerge from the school vision. Lowe enhanced the multistep process to create the instructional vision by using the school vision as a foundation. He knew he was entering his new position with several blind spots; however, he was convinced that he could not lead the school's transformation effort without a clear instructional vision. Moreover, he knew that keeping staff focused on deliberate actions to teach each student well would be central to his work as the school's chief instructional leader.

To assess what staff were doing already to meet students' needs, Lowe examined data. He reviewed student achievement data; read teacher observations and evaluations and teacher lesson plans; held conversations with stakeholders (students, teachers, parents/guardians, district staff, and community members); surveyed stakeholders; analyzed the school's master schedule, teacher schedules, and resource staff schedules; reviewed behavior intervention programs; studied the professional development schedule; looked at staff attendance records and team meeting notes; and read leadership team meeting notes. He also realized that previous efforts had resulted in teacher burnout, student frustration, parent/community disengagement, and overall low school morale. He knew the work had to be very detailed, but that he had to stick with it to do what was needed for the students.

He observed:

- Daily instruction appeared to be teacher centered. Most activities seemed to be whole group and lacked authentic effort to engage students.
- Daily instruction did not appear to be differentiated based on student learning needs. There was little to no evidence of any preassessment to determine appropriate instructional entry points.
- Daily instruction often concluded with little to no assessment of student learning, and there was little to no evidence that teachers made adjustments based on the ongoing use of assessment data.
- Daily instruction appeared to be based simply on "getting through the curriculum" and not on ensuring that students learned.
- Daily instruction demonstrated minimal evidence of responding to differences in student performance patterns.
- Daily instruction and daily use of purchased interventions seemed so interconnected that it was difficult to know whether daily instruction occurred prior to using the interventions.
- There was no evidence that teacher professional development changed practice.
- There was no evidence that teacher professional development changed student outcomes.

Since he was new, Lowe did not share his observations with the staff. Instead, he used his observations to create his initial equity-focused instructional vision. His instructional vision would be revised based on data collected throughout the year; however, it was the guiding light for his work beginning the first day of the teacher duty week. (Figure 3.4 may be used as a frame for this work.)

Lowe's Equity-Focused Instructional Vision

I will use my leadership skills, my commitment to doing what is best for students daily, and my unfettered belief that we, school administrators and teachers, are life-long learners focused on maximizing student achievement to ensure the following:

1. High-quality instruction occurs in every classroom every day. ALL teachers will plan lessons using the lesson plan template agreed upon by the faculty. The template requires teachers to outline how they will adjust lessons for various student learners without compromising the grade-level standard. Specific emphasis on data used to determine entry points to engage students is essential.

Metric of Success:

- 100 percent of teachers will engage in professional learning to ensure they understand the lesson plan template and all components.
- 100 percent of teachers will have written lessons plans in the requisite format.
- 100 percent of teachers will implement lessons as intended with multiple learners in mind and without compromising the rigor of the grade-level standard.

2. Teachers are provided requisite resources (materials, time, and support) to focus on planning for high-quality "first instruction" on a daily basis. ALL teachers will implement their lessons using curricular resources, current student classroom data, additional adult support, technological tools, and digital resources to provide student-centered instruction. *First instruction* is defined as instruction delivered for the first time to students. Teachers should be focused on becoming experts in providing high-quality first instruction rather than experts in interventions for students who "do not get it."

Metric of Success:

- 100 percent of teachers will adhere to the core instructional program for each student.
- 100 percent of teachers will use instructional resources to provide daily core instruction aligned with the appropriate grade-level standards.
- 100 percent of teachers will use less than 20 percent of their daily classroom instruction on teacher-directed activity.
- 100 percent of teachers will adjust their instruction based on disaggregated student achievement data.
- 100 percent of teachers will analyze disaggregated student achievement data to create personalized pathways for students to exceed grade-level expectations.
- 100 percent of teachers will use disaggregated preassessment data to determine appropriate entry points for daily instruction.
- 100 percent of teachers will capture students' voices to adjust instructional practices based on what the students share works best for them (primary students can provide input in small groups; intermediate and secondary students can participate in small-group discussions and can complete surveys).

3. Teachers participate in equity learning cycles focused on a critical examination of daily observable practices in our classes.

Metric of Success:

- 100 percent of equity learning cycles will follow the equity learning cycle protocol (described more fully later in the chapter).
- 100 percent of teachers will participate in learning cycles and journal their experience, and they will bring artifacts to collaborative planning sessions to document their change in practice based on the professional development provided.
  - ○ Artifacts represent students in each student group. Analysis will be based on asking the critical question "What does student X need to meet and then exceed the grade-level standard?"
- Disaggregated student assessment data of first instruction material will increase by 50 percent or more each quarter with the first quarter scores (if skills or recursive), preassessment, and/or diagnostic assessment data serving as baseline data.

4. A school culture is developed in which stakeholders are encouraged to share their struggles, frustrations, and successes with the ultimate goal of being focused on student outcomes.

Metric of Success:

- 100 percent of staff will complete monthly surveys to capture perception data. Trend data and all comments will be shared at the first leadership meeting of the month. This information will then be reported in the second "week at a glance" for the month. An administrative response to trend data will be provided.
- 100 percent of staff will participate in quarterly reflection meetings with the principal. In addition to emergent agenda items, staff will provide updated data on their performance goals and student achievement data (disaggregated by student group and grade-level expectations). Instructional adjustments and next steps will be addressed.

5. I am the chief learner in the school community, and all adults will partner with me as we engage in this incredible work of learning together. Our students' success depends on our partnership, and we have no time to spare.

Metric of Success:

- A member of the administrative team will attend all collaborative planning sessions.
- A member of the administrative team will attend all equity learning cycles.
- I will teach at least one class every other week using strategies discussed at collaborative planning. Teachers will be invited to observe and brainstorm with me regarding how to enhance practice.
- Focused "learning walks" will occur every two weeks and include classroom teachers, principals, assistant principals, school-based resource staff, central office resource staff, and/or consultants. Observations from these walks will be discussed at each collaborative planning session.

6. We stay focused on doing this work well before we commence any new initiatives. We define our progress, in large part, based on student performance outcomes; however, perception and observation data will also inform our work.

(Continued)

(Continued)

Metric of Success:

- No new initiatives will commence this year.
- 100 percent of our success will be defined in terms of student outcomes. (Teachers will define their progress in delivering high-quality first instruction using student formative and summative assessment data.)

My commitment to high-quality first instruction in every classroom will be evidenced by my observing instruction at least three hours a day. These observations will inform upcoming collaborative planning agendas and other professional development sessions.

Lowe's equity-focused instructional vision reflected what he gleaned from data. He used his instructional vision to remain focused on priorities, and he monitored daily what he expected. He used what he saw to shape collaborative planning agendas and job-embedded professional development and to decide how to use nonteaching resource staff. Throughout the year, he took notes on what changes he would need to make in the master schedule, personnel, and budget for the upcoming school year. He used his first year to collect data and have conversations about instruction needed for students.

The Master Schedule Supports an Equity-Focused Instructional Vision

Creating the master schedule is a task frequently delegated to an assistant principal or, in some instances, a teacher leader. The master schedule, however, is the linchpin necessary for a school community to make meaningful adjustments to increase student achievement for each student. There is an equity imperative to ensure that each student receives *quality first instruction.* We define quality first instruction as daily exposure to the core instructional program with differentiated pathways for each student to meet the learning target. Furthermore, the instructional program should include embedded opportunities during the school day for each student to preview material, have material retaught in a different fashion, and/or have the new learning extended and enriched. Scheduling students with educational gaps, English language acquisition goals, and special needs *first*, for example, ensures from the beginning of the school year that traditionally marginalized students are positioned to experience academic success. Carefully assigning teachers to specific student groups involves thought and honest reflection. Who is being assigned to the most vulnerable student groups?

Figure 3.4	Initial Thinking Guiding the Creation of an Equity-Focused Instructional Vision	
Instructional Areas (Organize your responses by stakeholder groups)	**Now**	**Preferred Future**
STUDENTS		
Student outcomes (hard and soft data)		
Student accountability for their learning (student-managed data folders, metacognitive journaling, and student-led parent conferences)		
Culture of high expectations for each student		
Others:		
TEACHERS		
Daily first instruction		
Student engagement and comprehension surveys to inform teaching practices		
Staff's ability to diagnostically assess and then adjust instruction accordingly		
Staff turnover		
School climate		
Culture of high expectations for each student (evaluation of who is being given "stretch" activities and exposure to above-grade-level material/courses)		
Job-embedded, differentiated professional development		
Use of intervention only after quality first instruction		
Use of data to drive daily instruction (student work, daily formative assessments, summative assessments, benchmarks, etc.)		
Analysis of data by gaps between student groups and within student groups		
Whole-to-part instruction (differentiation and fluid small-group instruction)		
Others:		
PARENTS		
Culture of high expectations for each student		
Others:		

Principals need to have courageous conversations with staff about class assignments. Students with academic challenges are often assigned to less veteran staff members who have not yet developed the skills needed to meet the instructional goals of diverse learners. A developing teacher may use the curriculum as a directive rather than a guide to integrating skills, creating rather than closing instructional gaps. Sometimes this is repeated several times in a student's educational career.

When Vicki Goodfield reported to her new assignment as principal, the master schedule had already been created and teachers had been given their assignments. When she studied the schedule, Goodfield found that the department chairpersons, presumably the school's best teachers, were teaching the gifted and talented and honors classes at each grade level. The students in these classes (and their parents) were more involved, so the reasoning was that the more experienced teachers needed to be assigned to those students. One chairperson said, "The students in the lower-level courses just sit there, and their parents don't call or come to the school. It's easier for a new teacher to be assigned to those classes." The student achievement data showed that students in the advanced and honors classes outperformed students in the lower-level classes by 20 percent to 30 percent on local and state interim and end-of-year assessments.

Goodfield knew that staff members needed to shift their mindsets about who taught what, but she did not want to damage the trust she was building with her team. She called a leadership team retreat to review the data and reflect. When the department chairpersons recognized that the patterns were not in their students' best interests, they took charge of the three lowest-performing classes at each grade level. The leadership team agreed to collect data on teaching practices and student outcomes. The master schedule became the cornerstone of equity work within the schoolhouse.

Scheduling for Optimal Learning Opportunities

Principals usually are efficient at instituting organized practices; however, design of the master schedule does not always reflect creativity and flexibility in using resources effectively and efficiently by maximizing time on task, using space appropriately, and thoughtfully assigning staff to student groups (Spear, 1992). Responding to diverse students' instructional and emotional needs requires alternative scheduling. Three types of flexible schedules are block, rotating, and dropped. The literature is full of examples of each; however, a brief description of each follows.

Block schedules are typically found in middle and high schools. The block time is used for interdisciplinary teams and consists of two or more combined periods. The combined periods can be used for multiple purposes, including project-based learning; mathematics and science instruction by the same teacher; language arts and social studies instruction by the same teacher; extracurricular activities; or extended-learning-time opportunities for each student (Benevino, Snodgrass, Adams, & Dengel, 1999). The block schedule also allows for alternate-day classes. For example, a student could take technology classes on Mondays, Wednesdays, and Fridays and then take an extended-learning-time class on Tuesdays and Thursdays.

Rotating schedules are flexible schedules with classes held at different times each day. Based on the belief that many students learn best in the morning, the rotating schedule allows students to take all classes during the morning hours at some time during the week (Canady & Rettig, 1995). For example, a student could take language arts at 8 a.m. on Monday, 9 a.m. on Tuesday, 10 a.m. on Wednesday, and so on. Also, rotating schedules provide some variety for the instructional staff that may be worthwhile.

Dropped schedules involve having more classes than actual periods in a given school day. The goal is to have one class dropped each day so that schedules provide for instruction such as independent reading with individual student conferencing, study skills instruction, project-based learning, and reteaching of lessons in specific or interdisciplinary courses. The first or last period of the day can be dropped to include one of these instructional efforts (Canady & Rettig, 1995; Curtis & Bidwell, 1977).

Some school districts may dictate the type of schedule to be used by level: elementary, middle, or high. Principals must be creative and make decisions within their control to address achievement challenges. Providing extended-learning-time opportunities is critical. These opportunities could take the form of a morning reteaching club, a Lunch Bunch literature group, an after-school tutoring program, a Saturday learning workshop, or a fixed or floating period during the school day. Although some scholars prefer one type of extended-learning-time format over another, the best such opportunities are those that occur *during the school day*, to ensure that *each* student benefits from the effort. The most beneficial opportunity for teachers and students is to have a designated time during the school day when teachers can focus on providing quality instruction that includes addressing missing skills and enriching students using on-grade-level materials. Including this time in the master schedule, along with a plan for teaching and learning during this extended time, is important. Some schools name this time zero period, enrichment period, reteach period, or multitiered instruction period. Whatever the name of this time, master schedules are more responsive to students' needs when they are created with the goal of providing full access to high-quality core instruction combined with an intentional strategy to address students who have skills gaps, as well as those students who need to be stretched (Rocha, 2007).

An elementary school principal, for example, could use block schedules to integrate into the master schedule a readers' workshop with individual student conferencing. Teachers would have time then to (a) build students' independent reading skills, (b) assess students' comprehension and fluency skills to make appropriate instructional adjustments, and (c) provide supplemental support (by the teacher of record, another teacher, or the reading specialist). A parallel structure for mathematics could include opportunities for teachers to provide small-group instruction coupled with built-in time for fluid regrouping between classes based on students' understanding of specific skills. Students who needed more intensive support could receive push-in instruction without missing any core instruction time. Principals should assess their schools' needs collaboratively with stakeholders (students, teachers, parents/guardians, and district-level administrators) to determine what is best for the school community.

Student Engagement

Time is one of the most precious resources in the teaching and learning dynamic. Principals need to make judicious choices about scheduling to support and maximize opportunities for students to learn. Scheduling is the foundation of that support. But building the optimal schedule will not make a difference without daily quality teaching and learning. Student engagement needs to be addressed concurrently with scheduling decisions. The school leader is driven by three fundamental questions in analyzing engagement:

1. What do students need in order to be engaged in teaching and learning at this school?

2. What do teachers know about their students that will lay the foundation for authentic engagement?

3. What do teachers know about student engagement and what do they do to stimulate and maintain students' active engagement?

In asking what students need in order to be engaged in teaching and learning, a principal should consider students' voices in describing what involves them in schoolwork, both in the larger organization as well as in the classroom. However, school staff rarely take into consideration what students want as a regular component of their educational experience. Information gathered from students should be organized according to overarching themes. Students will, no doubt, tell us what we already know about their engagement needs, but taking the time to ask is essential. They will tell us that they want learning to be fun. They want to move around and have hands-on experiences. They want to discuss. They want smart, caring teachers. Perhaps the issue is not the getting of feedback, but what principals do with the feedback they get.

According to Fredricks, Blumenfeld, and Paris (2004), student engagement can be characterized as cognitive, behavioral, and emotional. Cognitive engagement is a student's *investment* in the attending demand of an activity. Behavioral engagement is a student's *participation* in the learning activity. Emotional engagement is the student's *affective relationship* in the educational process. Clearly students need to be involved if we are to make the best use of time for learning. Which brings us to our second question: What do teachers know about student engagement, and what do they do to stimulate and maintain students' active engagement? To engage students in twenty-first-century learning, teachers can use technology to enhance lesson design and implementation; to individualize, differentiate, and/or personalize learning; to provide a platform for collaborating with peers, teachers, and the larger community; and to offer students choice in the learning process. Too often teachers remain focused on students coming quickly into the classroom and starting an assignment, having a pen or pencil, having a written pass if arriving late or leaving early, and other common routines, limiting other forms of student-teacher relationships (Jensen, 2009).

Engaging students emotionally makes a significant difference, particularly for students from diverse backgrounds and students who have experienced academic underachievement. One middle school principal, for example, reviewed interim assessment data with teachers and asked teachers to declare a corrective teaching plan during quarterly teacher data meetings. The teachers then took the quarterly data meetings to the next level by adding students' voices. After the teacher data conversations, students engaged in roundtable discussions with teachers about what they felt teachers could do differently to engage the students and positively impact student outcomes. Prior to the roundtable, the school counselors selected a sample of students (student athletes, student council members, National Junior Honor Society members, cafeteria helpers, and other informal leaders in the school). The school counselors reviewed the questions, the protocol for the day, and helped to create a safe place for the students. Once in the student data review meeting, the counselors asked questions and recorded students' responses (without recording individual students' names) and shared the information with teachers. The principal asked the teachers to go back to their plans and adjust them in response to the student feedback. After the revisions, the principal reviewed each plan and created a monitoring tool to assess whether teachers implemented plans with fidelity.

UNDERSTANDING THE TEACHING AND LEARNING DYNAMIC

The best way to understand the teaching and learning dynamic is to observe instruction as often as possible. However, to get a full and complete understanding, leaders need to cross-reference instructional observations with other data sources, such as student work, district-wide or schoolwide formative and summative assessments, feedback from instructional rounds, and/or stakeholder discussion groups. The information-gathering process should focus on the principal's instructional vision, but the original vision should always be subject to revision so that it is responsive to any gaps that current or new data identify.

What Is Seen and Heard in the Classroom

Observing the teaching and learning dynamic is a meaningful experience if principals commit daily uninterrupted time to observing instruction using an equity lens. Some district leaders require principals to spend a certain percentage of their workday in classrooms, but in addition to being in classrooms routinely, principals also need to provide teachers with meaningful feedback, preferably within 24–48 hours of the visitation. Tools that can record feedback digitally can help principals look for trends across teachers, grade levels, and content areas. GoObserve, LoTi Observer, or iWalkthrough Classroom Observation, for example, help principals to mine data by identifying themes and patterns from walkthroughs. Some school districts may have purchased licenses with other vendors or created their own internal tools. Regardless of the tool used, principals should not analyze the data manually, if possible. Figure 3.5 outlines process considerations for analyzing themes. These considerations should be made *before* observations are undertaken, to ensure that the observations provide the needed information. Figure 3.6 shows a sample teaching and learning snapshot. This form could be used, for example, if a specific online tool or app is not used. Figure 3.7 highlights some of the teaching practices and indicators of student success that might be compiled from a series of observations.

Figure 3.5	Theme Analysis Across Grades and Contents

1. Does your visitation schedule enable you to capture authentic teacher and student exchanges across grades and content areas?
   a. How frequently do you observe instruction to assess if the curriculum is being implemented across grades and content areas?
   b. How is pacing across grades and content areas?
2. Does your visitation schedule include multiple opportunities to have different qualified observers visit different classrooms?
   a. How frequently are different observers visiting classes?
   b. Is there an opportunity for different observers to reflect together regarding the same instructional observation?
3. Does your visitation process include frequent opportunities for observation findings to be reviewed collectively and individually?
   a. What is your process for providing feedback to teachers regarding instructional adjustments that can be made, based on observations?
   b. How do you follow up to see if adjustments have been made?

The teaching and learning snapshot process is a tool for the principal and the teacher being observed. Principals learn about their teachers, their students, their school environment, and themselves through focused observations of teacher instructional practices linked to evidence of student learning. Observing and examining authentic student work is essential to understanding the teaching and learning dynamic (see Figure 3.8). Principals can select a simple protocol to use as part of the walkthrough; however, the protocol must identify which children are sitting in which classes and how students are grouped generally. After the walkthrough, the tuning protocol (Blythe et al., 1999) is a simple, consistent process for examining student work in collaborative biweekly meetings. The principal may use a series of uniform questions for observation, given that student work will supplement the teaching and learning snapshot.

In addition to observation and examining student work, principals can organize schoolwide visitations with colleagues from other school communities and members of the district's curriculum and instruction offices to enhance their understanding of the teaching and learning dynamic. City, Elmore, Fiarman, and Teitel (2009) describe a powerful interschool visitation protocol called *instructional rounds*. Many principals are familiar with some type of interschool visitation model; however, the instructional rounds process provides a consistent, nonthreatening way to engage in a collaborative visitation process.

Instructional rounds include four elements: a problem of practice, observation of practice, observation debrief, and next level of work (City et al., 2009).

Figure 3.6   Teaching and Learning Snapshot

Teacher's Name	
Date	
Time (start and end)	
Grade/Course	
Observer/s	
Teaching and Learning Focus (if applicable)	
Teaching Practices	Evidence of student learning (Note any differences in learning engagement/disengagement. Use diversity factors in notes.):
Highly Effective Teaching Practice/ Transfer of Professional Development (PD) to the Classroom	Evidence of effective teaching practice (Clearly note any distinctions for every student group.): Evidence of transfer of past PD into changed teacher practice (Clearly note past PD and if it related to any specific student group.):
PD Implication (if any)	Student Work Collected: Yes or No (If yes, what was collected, and what trends in performance were noted?)
Teacher's Response	
Follow-Up Discussion Requested (by school leader or teacher)	Yes No Requested by_____
Follow-Up Discussion Date (if held)	

Note: This snapshot is presented in open-ended format rather than as a checklist to provide more authentic data that better reflect the teaching and learning process.

Figure 3.7 Sample Teaching Practices and Indicators of Student Learning

Sample Teaching Practices	*Sample Indicators of Student Learning**
• Teacher provides explicit instruction for reading strategies (before, during, and after). • Teacher models explicit instruction for reading strategies. • Teacher provides guided practice for reading strategies. • Teacher uses student conferencing to assess students' reading skills. • Teacher engages students by using data gleaned from student interest survey. • Teacher uses culturally relevant text to engage students. • Teacher uses manipulatives (e.g., real-world objects and scientific artifacts) to teach concrete mathematical skills. • Teacher uses models to teach mathematical skills. • Teacher uses whole-to-part instruction to teach a new skill. • Teacher uses formative assessment data to adjust the lesson (e.g., varied class work, small-group assignments, pacing adjustments). • Teacher uses technology to engage and/or differentiate (e.g., InterWrite slates, all-student-response system, flip camera). • Teacher uses four corners, philosophical chair, differentiated centers, and the like to extend and refine learning authentically. • Teacher tiers questioning (knowledge, comprehension, application, analysis, synthesis, and evaluation) to engage students in higher-order thinking. • Teacher uses nonlinguistic representations (e.g., drama, videos, graphic organizers). • Teacher uses leveled reading materials to meet students' individual learning needs.	• Students are engaged in meaningful student-to-student conversations regarding the content material. • Students are engaged in meaningful student-to-teacher conversations. • Students answer higher-order thinking questions with evidence of understanding. • Students present higher-order thinking questions to the teacher for reflection and refinement of the new content material. • Students' written responses are aligned with the teacher's assignment rubric and content standards. • Students make transdisciplinary connections. • Students apply new learning to authentic scenarios in and out of the classroom setting. • Students demonstrate content mastery by simulations, role playing, performances, debates, discussions, demonstrations, etc. • Students chart their own progress toward content standards using individual learning goals tools. • Students apply learning through the creation of a scientific model, poem, original story, etc. • Students critique the day's lesson and/or media clip accurately. • Students answer an end-of-class multiple-choice assessment accurately. • Students answer an end-of-class exit ticket accurately. • Students summarize the new learning and connect it appropriately to information presented in a previous lesson. • Students peer edit material accurately.

*These indicators for student learning are performance based and mastery based. They can be augmented as schools and school systems enhance their state curricula to extend beyond the Common Core State Standards. As observations of student learning are noted, differences in student responses should be included.

Figure 3.8   Sample Questions to Guide a School Leader's Independent
Review of Student Work

Evidence of Student Thinking	Evidence of Effective Teaching Practices
• Did the student attempt to answer the question? • Did the student expressly connect the answer to text? • Did the student expressly connect the answer to a nontext instructional resource (e.g., a media source)? • Did the student connect an outside personal experience to the answer? • Did the student use an example to answer the question? • Did the student demonstrate a complete understanding of the material presented? • Did the student respond using literal or complex reasoning? • Did the student stay on topic?	• Did the student use a technique shared in class by the teacher or a peer? Is there evidence that a previous lesson enhanced the student's response? • Did the student use content-appropriate vocabulary? • Did the student follow the directions outlined in the assignment? • Did the student connect the response to any teaching material (e.g., textbook, PowerPoint, content-related poster, teacher website, teacher-created handout)?

To establish instructional rounds, principals need commitment from a diverse network of educators, a collaborative relationship with other schools that also will conduct instructional rounds, expectations for the network of professionals engaging in the instructional rounds, and the dedication to devote at least two days a month to engage in instructional rounds (City et al., 2009).

Leaders must make these visitations nonevaluative and supportive in order to enhance teachers' professional capacities, regardless of the type of observation they ultimately elect to use. It is also helpful to have professionals connected to the school and from outside the school community share their insights before and after interschool and intraschool visitations. For example, one principal who wanted to give teachers constructive feedback outside of evaluation created a principal's advisory group with teacher representatives from each grade and every content area. At the first advisory meeting, he shared data and the team analyzed strengths and weaknesses by grade and content area without using teachers' names. The team identified general themes by grade level and content area. The advisory group then created a protocol for how the leadership team would support teachers and agreed to meet quarterly to review real-time observation data. The team also agreed that the leadership team would revisit the job-embedded professional development calendar, as needed.

You might be thinking, "So, what is new about all of this?" We are proposing that you incorporate a series of critical questions to dig deeper into the instructional rounds process (see Figure 3.9). We call these critical questions an *equity learning protocol*. When we embed this protocol into the established infrastructure of instructional rounds or any other visitation structure, we see the work evolve into equity learning cycles.

Figure 3.9 Equity Learning Protocol

Before the Visitation

1. The school principal, or his or her designee, describes the context for the visit. Provide specific information regarding the problem of practice, the focus topic for the walk, expectations for collecting observations, and the like. Underscore data that are relevant to each student group.
2. Provide visitation participants with a walkthrough tool (hard copy or electronic) to align their feedback to the problem of practice or focus topic for the walk.
3. Divide visitation participants into prearranged groups to ensure diversity of content and perspectives.
4. Review the equity dialogue process to be used during the visitation debriefing: (a) set the tone (e.g., "We are here to grow and learn from your observations and understand your observation is based on a snapshot in time. Direct and honest feedback is appreciated."); (b) state the intent of the visit; (c) give specific examples of observations (e.g., "In the 9th grade algebra class, there were 20 students, of which 16 were male and 19 were non-white. All students worked on problems independently."); (d) note activities of all students and specific student groups; (e) describe behavior that suggests the teacher made explicit learning decisions with diverse learners in mind (evidence of differentiated materials for various learning styles, deliberate schema building, evidence of accommodations made for students with special education and linguistic needs, etc.); (f) describe behavior that indicates the teacher made an intentional effort to make the learning relevant; (g) note evidence that the teacher attempted to engage students authentically (student choice, student surveys, authentic student-to-student conversations regarding the content, etc.); and (h) note any variations between all students and specific student groups.
5. Provide visitation participants with a map of the building (with grade and content listed) and parameters for the visit: length of the entire visitation, time to be spent in each classroom, debriefing location, any direction regarding hallway mini-debriefs, and directions regarding how participants should conduct themselves during the classroom visitations (stand in the rear of the room, sit with students, talk to students, etc.).

During the Visitation

6. Visitation participants should take notes using the visitation template provided and note specific observations relative to students.

After the Visitation: The Debrief

7. The school principal, or his or her designee, describes the authentic dialogue process to guide the debrief session. First, review the elements of the equity

(Continued)

Figure 3.9   *(Continued)*

dialogue process: (a) set the tone, (b) state the intent of the visit, (c) give specific examples of observations, (d) note activities of all students and specific student groups, (e) describe behavior that suggests the teacher made explicit learning decisions with diverse learners in mind, (f) describe behavior that indicates the teacher made an intentional effort to make the learning relevant, (g) note evidence that the teacher attempted to engage students authentically, and (h) note any variations between all students and specific student groups.

8. Ask visitation groups to share their reflections. If the walkthrough tool was not electronic, the school principal, or his or her designee, should delegate someone to take notes during the debriefing. (Some participants may not be comfortable giving their notes to the school; therefore, taking notes during the debriefing is strongly encouraged.)

Note: Use the information from the debrief to inform whole-school, department, and/or individual professional development. Provide the staff with a written snapshot-in-time summary (without names).

The goal is to unpack every aspect of the visitation process using the equity learning protocol to promote equity at the onset and throughout the visitation. The equity learning protocol can be used to transform any existing visitation structure into an equity learning cycle.

Beyond What Is Seen and Heard in the Classrooms

The PACE Framework asks educators to review formative and summative assessments, but *only* as a snapshot in time. Educators must cross-reference multiple data sources to gain a holistic understanding of the teaching and learning dynamic (Bernhardt, 2008; Ellis, 2001). Principals become accustomed to examining several data sources to identify themes, patterns, and outliers, an invaluable skill for attempting to reverse achievement gap trends. Stakeholders' voices also are critical, and principals are encouraged to have three focus group discussions: one for teachers, one for students, and one for parents/guardians. Although quarterly discussions are recommended, it may be more feasible to have focus group discussions each semester. Participants in each group should be a diverse sample of the stakeholder population and should rotate (Krueger, 1988). For teachers and students, consider meeting before or after school and offering light refreshments. It may be more challenging getting parents into school, so consider scheduling the discussions before popular evening events, such as back-to-school night, parent-teacher conference nights, student award assemblies, winter and spring concerts, art nights, athletic events, or the like. As an alternative to an in-person focus group discussion, consider a cyber-meeting, such as a collaborative wiki, a virtual conference, a secure chat room discussion, or a Skype talk. If none of these options is feasible, a telephone conference call may be a viable alternative. By cross-referencing information gleaned from the teaching and learning snapshot, student work, districtwide and/or schoolwide formative and summative assessments, instructional rounds feedback, and focus group discussions, principals should have a complete understanding of the teaching and learning dynamic.

At this point, educators may need to refine their vision for the teaching and learning dynamic to reflect what they have learned. Again, the purpose of creating an equity-focused instructional vision is not only to describe the school's teaching and learning goals, but also to share a plan of action to help all staff display the behaviors outlined in the instructional vision. Leaders have the difficult task of creating a quality program for all students and ensuring that students excel on a snapshot-in-time test, as required by federal legislation. Effective public school principals create and institutionalize a sound instructional program for each student. If leaders are effective, students will be able to demonstrate the skills assessed by teacher, school, local, state, and federal performance accountability systems. Although the PACE Framework does not specifically address each state's assessment, when each student has access to a quality instructional program on a daily basis, students will meet performance goals and achievement gaps will close.

Principals have two roles—to ensure that quality teaching and learning are occurring daily and to meet the goals set out for local and state standardized assessments. PACE addresses both roles. Figure 3.10 lists questions that principals should consider when checking for students' acquisition of knowledge, skills, and processes aligned with the core curriculum. This process relates to the *assessment* of the teaching and learning dynamic, the second aspect of the PACE Framework.

Figure 3.10   The Dual Roles of Public School Principals

1. Is your core instructional program aligned with college *and* workforce readiness?
2. Do you use a response-to-instruction model that promotes quality instruction, not just interventions? Please note the intentional use of language. Much has been said about response to *intervention*, but the focus here is on monitoring the quality of daily instruction, which is framed as response to *instruction.*
   a. How do you ensure that instruction is adjusted based on students' needs?
   b. What process do you employ to ensure teachers have a robust instructional tool kit?
3. What internal monitoring processes do you use to document students' acquisition of skills?
   a. Does your monitoring process include a monitoring tool?
   b. If so, how frequently do you review the monitoring tool?
   c. What is your response to information gleaned from the monitoring tool?

PROFESSIONAL DEVELOPMENT THAT CHANGES TEACHER PRACTICE

With the added challenges of teaching heterogeneous groups and adjusting to meet emerging standards, many, perhaps most, teachers are not equipped to negotiate their way alone through the teaching and learning dynamic. Principals can help by finding time for substantive job-embedded professional development. Teachers need time to reflect on their practice, collaborate with colleagues, examine student work by student groups, analyze formative and summative assessments by student groups to adjust their instruction, and engage in relevant job-embedded professional development.

The PACE Framework is built on the notions that *all* educators believe that *each* student can learn and that *all* educators believe they can develop the skills needed to reach *each* student. Put simply: This is the equity imperative. School leaders must address outliers, but the principles associated with this paradigm are based on what is possible, not impossible. DuFour et al. (2004) discuss how professional learning communities (PLCs) can be a catalyst to increasing student achievement, but the PLC designation is less important than the staff's engagement in collaborative, results-oriented, and equity-focused work. A school staff should be a group of professionals working in a culture of collaboration, support, and ongoing professional growth with the ultimate goal of educating *each* student well. Therefore, principals should establish a systematic forum to provide job-embedded professional development. Given what we know about PLCs, this format may be the best opportunity to create a systemic forum for your school community. We defer to the great work of DuFour et al. regarding establishing and maintaining quality PLCs. We encourage school leaders to explore how to build on this PLC work by using video to enhance authentic collaboration regarding day-to-day teaching practice. Phillips and Olson (2013) outline easy suggestions for integrating video to enhance the collaboration experience implicit in PLCs. Of course, school leaders should use a protocol that institutionalizes trust and assures teachers that this work is solely for teacher reflection and professional development (Phillips & Olson, 2013).

Creating, *Not* Waiting for, the Right Conditions

Principal Aisha Bell submitted three requests for additional staff during the summer, based on her prior year's enrollment and scheduled registrations, but given the severity of the district's budget cuts, she wasn't hopeful the requests would be met. She called in her leadership team to address the master schedule, predicting that the current staffing allocation would not align with the school's intervention model. Team members discussed writing letters to district leaders and asking the Parent-Teacher Association to get involved. Bell suggested revisiting the schedule to determine how it could be reconfigured to meet the needs of students as well as teachers.

Once Bell shifted the discussion, the team agreed that the best course would be to address the matter at the school level and they added a third class to each department chair's schedule. The additional class would serve as a job-embedded professional development classroom. Based on areas of need, the teaching strategies in the professional development classroom would vary. Teachers would receive release time, which would be granted on a rotating basis by members of an administrative and non-teaching resource team, to observe in the professional development classroom. The observation would be focused by teachers using a "look-for" tool, as well as several reflection questions that required the teachers to contrast what they were observing with their own practice. Department chairpersons and administrative team members would offer ongoing professional development to teachers in their charge, using feedback from quarterly data analysis meetings and professional development classroom observations to inform their conversations and to guide their next steps with each teacher. Bell acknowledged that the change would be taxing, but she believed it was essential to building the commitment necessary for creating a job-embedded learning environment.

The teaching and learning dynamic involves staff understanding effective instructional practices; using assessment data; aligning lesson plans with standards; implementing standards-based lessons; continually assessing students' interests and instructional needs; continually seeking ways to build meaningful relationships with students; and creating space to discuss issues of culture and how they influence the teaching and learning process. Therefore, optimal conditions must exist for teams to address teachers' varying capacities. Collaborative planning teams, grade-level teams, interdisciplinary teams, and content/department teams are essential. Teams also need the time to meet, and team meeting times should be nonnegotiable and integrated into the master schedule. These meetings allow professionals to engage in activities that focus on increasing student achievement. Teachers should be encouraged to continue to refine their craft in order to meet the increasingly complex needs of today's diverse learners. Experts stress that teachers' ongoing professional development should be embedded into the core of the teaching and learning dynamic (Darling-Hammond, 1996). Many teachers work part-time jobs, have young children at home, or attend school themselves, for instance, and principals cannot depend on strong voluntary, unpaid attendance (in nonunion states) at after-hours professional development. Putnam and Borko (2000) describe job-embedded professional development as learning that occurs on the school grounds during the school day, is connected to the teacher's work in the classroom, and uses real students and/or data. Officials in the U.S. Department of Education support such professional development, saying, "We believe the requirement to provide ongoing, high quality, job-embedded professional development to staff in a school is clearly tied to improving instruction in multiple ways" (U.S. Department of Education, 2009, p. 58479).

Job-embedded professional development can take many forms, including examining student work, lesson study, peer reflection, data teams, coaching, case study discussions, action research, and mentoring (Croft, Coggshall, Dolan, Powers, & Killion, 2010). In Chapter 6, we discuss how to implement the PACE Framework in a school community. However, PACE cannot be implemented in a school community that does not have the proper conditions in place. It should not be implemented after a master schedule has been created, for example. In that case, the school leader should consider building awareness about professional learning and building consensus around a few strategies. Principals may ask for volunteer teachers to participate in "no-fault" professional development. By doing so, principals are building the volunteers' background knowledge and potentially establishing cheerleaders for the work to be done in the upcoming school year.

Professional development should be relevant and validate participants' experiences. Modifying professional development based on evaluation feedback also is critical (Guskey, 2000). All professional development sessions should conclude with an evaluation. Evaluation data should be reviewed, analyzed, and used to adjust subsequent professional development sessions. Figure 3.11 is a sample professional development evaluation. With job-embedded professional development, school leaders must look for evidence of the transfer of professional learning into changed teacher behavior. That outcome depends on several variables, including the following:

- The complexity of the content presented at the professional development session
- Teachers' perceptions about whether or not the new learning is relevant
- The resources in place to provide structure as teachers experience successes and challenges during the implementation period

Figure 3.11   Sample Professional Development Evaluation

Job-Embedded Professional Development Evaluation

1. To what extent was your time well spent?

    a. The information was useful.

Useful				Not Very Useful
5	4	3	2	1

    b. The material made sense.

Made Sense				Did Not Make Sense
5	4	3	2	1

2. To what extent did you obtain the knowledge and skills identified in the objectives?

    a. Reviewing and identifying the implications of **X**

Completely				Not at All
5	4	3	2	1

    b. Practicing **X**, if applicable

Completely				Not at All
5	4	3	2	1

3. To what extent do you expect that you will be able to apply effectively in your school the new knowledge and skills you have acquired in these sessions?

A Great Deal				Not at All
5	4	3	2	1

4. In what specific ways will you apply your learning today in your classroom?
5. For the purpose of planning for future professional development sessions related to implementing **X**, what other topics would you like to explore?

Note: Evaluation questions suggested by Guskey (2000).

- Teachers' perceptions of how the new learning logically connects to their existing understanding of the teaching and learning dynamic
- The time and space to explore, without evaluation, the implementation of the new learning acquired in the professional development session (Darling-Hammond, 1996; Ferraro, 2000; Guskey, 2002)

Figures 3.12 and 3.13 provide artifacts for determining changed teacher behavior resulting from the professional development session and data sources for determining the transfer of professional learning to classroom instruction. Professional development should be meaningful, connected to teachers' daily work, deliberately connected to issues of equity and access, committed to translating theory to practice, and aimed at embedding the work within the context of the job (i.e., job-embedded instruction). The effectiveness of the professional development should be assessed, the teachers' ability to transfer the professional development into changed behavior should be determined, and principals should collect data to determine whether student outcomes have been positively impacted.

CONCLUSION

Experience, work in the field, and several bodies of literature support implementation of the PACE Framework as an effective process, not only to improve achievement for each student but to transform the teaching and learning dynamic within any public school. The PACE Framework may seem like common sense; however, common sense is not always common. Others may think PACE is complex or even overwhelming. Those who find it challenging might step back and reflect.

Figure 3.12	Sample Types of Data to Assess Effectiveness of Professional Development
Strategies for Assessing the Professional Development Session	*Strategies for Assessing Changed Teacher Behavior Resulting From the Professional Development Session*
• Questionnaires • Observations of participants' interactions and conversation during the professional development • Individual interviews • Focus group interviews • Instructor's anecdotal notes	• Classroom observations • Teacher reflection logs • Teacher portfolio (sample teacher-created lessons, assessments, and student work assignments) • Student portfolio (sample student work) • Assessments (if the professional development was content focused)

Figure 3.13   Checklist of Data Sources to Assess Transfer of Professional Development

☐ Explicit use of the professional development strategy, technique, practice, technology, etc.
☐ Implicit use of the professional development strategy, technique, practice, technology, etc. (partial use observed)
☐ Teacher's planning book, notes, unit plan, etc. that indicate an attempt to integrate the professional development strategy, technique, practice, technology, etc.
☐ Teacher's reflection journal that indicates an attempt to integrate the professional development strategy, technique, practice, technology, etc.
☐ Students' work samples that indicate that the professional development positively impacted the students' acquisition of skills or concepts
☐ Students' assessment data that indicate that the professional development positively impacted the students' acquisition of skills or concepts

PACE aligns with what we know from practice and literature must be done to *transform,* not simply *improve,* public schools. To do this work well, the transformation must be driven by an equity imperative with the understanding that this work does not involve a cookie-cutter approach, nor is it quick and easy. Instead, this work is complex and dynamic and requires adaptive leaders. School leaders will have to do things differently—perhaps not all things differently, but definitely some things differently. We know these ideas to be true:

• Our students' academic needs are diverse.
• Our teachers bring varying degrees of understanding of the teaching and learning dynamic to the schoolhouse.
• Our principals bring varying degrees of expertise to the leadership challenge for true transformation.
• Our school communities tend to be microcosms of the larger society.
• Principals are challenged to eliminate the persistent achievement gap trends with limited fiscal and human resources.
• Principals are charged with preparing *each* student, honoring demographic differences and learning needs, for the twenty-first century using an educational structure intended for white, middle-class students and a "sit and get" instructional delivery model.
• Some public school districts are not organized to provide valuable and relevant external support.

Most principals recognize these key ideas, but public schools generally are not organized, led, and supported to do the work of teaching *each* student well. In many public schools, school improvement (i.e., slightly adjusting programs, structures, and processes that contribute to the underperformance of certain students) is not enough to help the schools reach higher goals. Transforming the teaching and learning dynamic requires investing in human resources. The PACE Framework is a frame to guide principals through this work.

Underrepresented student groups, students from diverse backgrounds, students with disabilities, and poor students have been and continue to be underserved by America's public schools. We designed the PACE Framework to be a fluid process to assist principals as they contend with the challenge of confronting long-standing achievement gaps. Principals have the power to create conditions that will help more traditionally underserved groups of students experience academic success. However, their work continues to be dynamic as the browning of America occurs. Demographic trends reveal that, during the 2008–2050 period, the Hispanic population will approximately triple, from 46.7 million to 132.8 million; the African American population will surge from 41.1 million to 65.7 million; and the Asian population will grow from 15.5 million to 40.6 million (U.S. Census Bureau, 2008). Given the stubborn achievement gaps among various student groups, America's public schools are ripe for a paradigm shift that will assist principals in doing the work needed to ensure that each student is exposed to a quality instructional program on a daily basis.

Consequently, principals are urged to understand and, ultimately, broker the high-quality instructional challenge to move the work forward. We suggest that principals reflect honestly upon their own leadership skills, including an acknowledgment of gaps in their skills and/or knowledge competencies. Although many outside forces are shaping leaders' work, we can focus only on what we can control within the school—providing leadership that results in high-quality instruction. Effective principals must be humble enough to assess their skills constantly and ask, "What more can we learn to meet the academic needs of the students *currently* attending our schools?"

DISCUSSION QUESTIONS AND ACTIVITIES

1. Identify any tenet framing PACE that causes you to hesitate. What are your reservations? What tools do you have available to address your reservations?

2. Notwithstanding any external forces that affect your ability to implement PACE, what human resources within your school building can be accessed immediately to implement PACE? Consider conducting an audit of human resources for implementing PACE within your school community.

Part II
The Practice

4 The Leadership-for-Equity Dilemma

Principalship is the second greatest influence on student learning, second only to teacher effectiveness.

(Leithwood & Riehl, 2003)

The PACE Framework outlined in Chapter 3 provides a vital process for leading school transformation with equity as the key driver. The often unspoken truth, however, is that many school leaders were not trained or are not intuitively aware of how to lead for equity. Therefore, before we proceed with the discussion of how to implement the PACE framework (see Chapter 6), we want to pause and authentically analyze the *highly textured* and sometimes messy dilemmas associated with leading for equity.

Principals Janet Stacks, Jeffrey Dodge, and Elizabeth Springfield attended a summer leadership retreat. All three principals participated in a session titled "Overcoming Leadership Dilemmas." As a warm-up activity, the session facilitator asked the principals to identify one leadership dilemma they had experienced during the previous school year and then share how they had addressed the dilemma. Specifically, principals were asked to identify strategies used, resources reviewed, and/or individuals consulted when they shared how they addressed the dilemma. The warm-up activity revealed the following:

PRINCIPAL JANET STACKS

Dilemma: Over 70 percent of my teaching staff had three years or less of teaching experience. Therefore, we, the administrative team, spent a significant amount of time helping teachers with classroom management, strategies for conferencing effectively with parents, routines for daily homework, and tips for completing all the day-to-day tasks of teaching. Even though we were in year one of Common Core State Standards (CCSS) implementation, I never addressed unpacking the standards and reviewing the new CCSS reference material (even though this topic and information was shared in new teacher trainings). I was too busy to attend the training sessions since I needed to focus on creating an orderly building for all of my new teaching staff.

Addressing the Dilemma: I will provide more professional development related to high-impact lesson planning and implementation. Furthermore, I will commit to building my capacity regarding our district's transition to CCSS and require all administrators to become well versed in the transition as well. It is critical that I assist all staff and move beyond the nuts and bolts of day-to-day management tasks.

PRINCIPAL JEFFREY DODGE

Dilemma: There are so many district initiatives that I cannot manage them all. For example, we were asked to pilot a new third-grade science curriculum, teach a different math curriculum in kindergarten and first grade, and institute a literacy initiative throughout all grades. If that was not enough, we had a new teacher and administration system to implement. Oh, and in the midst of all this, I also had a new assistant principal, an underperforming administrative secretary, and a new supervisor.

Addressing the Dilemma: Honestly, I was simply overwhelmed. I applied for a few other jobs in the district, but I did not get anything. Therefore, I attempted to create a structure to delegate initiatives to various members of my leadership team. I was spinning in circles because I had no way to manage the new information myself or to manage a roll-out of the new information that varied per grade and, in some instances, content area.

PRINCIPAL ELIZABETH SPRINGFIELD

Dilemma: All African American, Hispanic, special education, and English language learner students consistently scored below proficiency on quarterly benchmark assessments. Teachers were trying to meet students' needs, but they kept saying, "We need more resources and interventions for these students."

Addressing the Dilemma: Teachers were not equipped with instructional toolkits to differentiate instruction for each student in their classrooms. Additionally, some teachers did not have an understanding of cultural competency, so they were challenged to relate to and connect with many students. Therefore, I collaborated with the district professional development office to provide a series of differentiation and cultural competency job-embedded professional development sessions. Also, the staff did a book study on culturally responsive instruction.

These principals' warm-up reflections highlight the three facets associated with the leadership-for-equity dilemma within the K–12 public education arena. We use the term *leadership-for-equity dilemma* to characterize the complexities associated with leading a public school in 2014 and beyond. The leadership-for-equity dilemma consists of three interrelated components:

1. Principal as an instructional leader for equity
2. Principal as a chief learner and change manager for equity
3. Principal as a facilitator of equity and access for each student

The leadership-for-equity dilemma captures the reality in which we, as public school educators, find ourselves as a record number of sitting principals are retiring, resigning, or seeking other education-related employment opportunities (Wallace Foundation, 2008). We believe that current professional development structures to enhance sitting principals' leadership skills are inadequate. Furthermore, we believe that there is an urgent need for the leadership-for-equity dilemma to be addressed (Stanford Educational Leadership Institute, 2007). To that end, we propose that school systems and/or school communities create a strategy to integrate a professional development plan that will confront the leadership-for-equity dilemma.

In this book, we assert that the traditional roles and expectations associated with principalship are, in large part, the silent noise in many schools and school districts. Our data tell us that what we are doing for all is not meeting the needs of many, but our work has yet to address how we adhere to the traditional job functions of the principalship while also leading for equity. In that vein, we will unpack the complexities linked with leading for equity and openly acknowledge this work is contextual, nuanced, and emerging. Using the principals' warm-up reflections as our frame, we will provide insights into and considerations for deliberately challenging the leadership-for-equity dilemma while contending with the day-to-day duties of principalship.

PRINCIPALS JANET STACKS AND JEFFREY DODGE: PRINCIPAL AS AN INSTRUCTIONAL LEADER FOR EQUITY, CHIEF LEARNER, AND CHANGE MANAGER FOR EQUITY

The notion that principals are instructional leaders has become standard commentary within the education arena. Therefore, we are often taken aback when we encounter sitting principals who do not have an instructional understanding of the current state standards, let alone an understanding of the newly adopted CCSS. During these encounters, we frequently ask ourselves the following questions:

- How do we support those who ascend to the principalship to lead for educational equity?
- Why aren't there more learning structures to enhance sitting principals' knowledge of equitable instructional practices that promote academic excellence for each student?

After asking ourselves these questions one too many times, we created a reflective questioning inventory designed to help principals realize potential growth opportunities related to instructional leadership for equity (see Figure 4.1). The Instructional Leadership for Equity Self-Inventory is adapted in form only, in part, from coaching structures developed by Costa and Garmston (2002). This inventory is designed to assist principals, like Stacks, examine their behavior, specifically inspecting the effectiveness of instructional programming for equity efforts. Let's consider how the inventory would be used with Stacks. She has a faculty of over 70 percent new staff (with fewer than three years of teaching experience), and she elected to spend an entire year working with staff solely on managerial skills. She proceeded with this work even though the district was implementing the CCSS. Other than the district's optional quarterly new teacher trainings, there were no other CCSS offerings for new teachers. Stacks stated that she was too busy to attend CCSS trainings and, ultimately, share her new learning with her staff. Furthermore, she did not discuss how "who the teachers are" intersects with "who the students are" to shape the teaching and learning dynamic (see Chapter 3). Stacks decided not to address the heart of teaching and learning, which is the quality of daily instruction for each student. Further, she did not provide new teachers with opportunities to relate their need for effective behavior management to the context of effective instruction. When there is high-quality, student-centered instruction, behavior management becomes a nonissue.

Figure 4.1	Instructional Leadership for Equity Self-Inventory

Reflective Questions	Instructional Leadership Exploration Areas
In your first 60 days as leader, how did you lead for equity? Provide specific examples that support your response.	**Assess Leadership Behavior** (Express understanding of behaviors; assessment is typically associated with a specific activity.)
Did you use your instructional vision for teachers when you created a plan of action for your new teachers? How did the instructional vision address equitable practices for staff and equitable outcomes for students?	**Relate Behaviors to Instructional Leadership** (Recollect how the assessment of leadership behaviors related specifically to instructional vision.)
Did your actions match your intended plan to lead for equity?	**Compare** (Draw a comparison between planned behavior and actual behavior.)
As you reflect on actions most and least related to the equity challenges in your school, consider the questions: What is getting in the way of your doing the work most pivotal to eliminating gaps in access to quality instruction? Given this information, what do you make of your actions? What facts, as you understood them, prompted you to proceed as you did?	**Infer** (Determine abstract meaning from data.)
What process did you use to monitor your work with new teachers?	**Metacognition** (Become aware of and monitor your own thinking during decision making.)
What inferences might you draw from your actions? Is there a disconnect between what you believe for each student and what is actually occurring?	**Infer From Data** (Draw hypotheses and explanations from the data provided.)
The following two items are tailored to Stacks's dilemma: What intuitions do you have to explain why you behaved as you did with your new teachers? How are you helping them to evolve into teachers who intentionally engage in daily culturally responsive teaching?	**Analyze** (Analyze data to determine if teachers achieved the goal[s] intended.)
Why did you not get the results with your new teachers that you had expected?	**Describe Cause and Effect** (Draw causal relationships.)
As you reflect on this inventory, what big ideas or insights are you discovering?	**Synthesize** (Make meaning from analysis of your behavior.)
As you plan future work with your new teachers, what insights have you developed that might be carried forth to the next school year?	**Apply** (Prescribe alternative approaches to the same work given the new insight gained.)
What specific assistance do you need to enhance your skills in instructional leadership for equity? What essential next steps are you going to take to enhance your instructional leadership skills?	**Evaluate** (Give feedback about the effects of this reflective questioning exchange.)

Objectively, we can see that she missed an opportunity for instructional leadership for equity; however, all principals find themselves faced with similar choices far too frequently. We designed the Instructional Leadership for Equity Self-Inventory to help principals make the right choices when it comes to instructional leadership.

Stacks's experience illustrates the first component of the leadership-for-equity dilemma: instructional leadership. Principals must stay abreast of instructional practices so that they can create conditions for professional growth within their staffs. Why was Stacks too busy to keep abreast of the new college and career standards, CCSS? Why was she more willing to provide training on managerial topics than on instructional topics focused on doing what is best for each student?

We contend that all principals desire to be instructional principals; however, the infrastructures needed to assist principals in evolving into instructional leaders are often fragmented or lacking. If you find that the necessary professional development structure is inadequate (or absent), you should do the following:

- Create a list of all of the major transformational efforts under way or expected in the near future in your district. Assess your ability to lead those efforts in your school community. Determine your growth areas, and create a plan to address those areas (see Figure 4.2).
- Join professional organizations (two to five, ideally) that provide printed, research-based journals.
- Attend professional development activities (two to five, ideally). (If fiscal resources are limited, consider attending local conferences or participating in free webinars.)
- Establish book study groups with fellow principals in your district.
- Maintain a professional journal to record your daily work, and use this journal to highlight areas in which you need additional support.
- Seek a mentor in the district office, higher education community, or larger education community who can serve as your mirror. You always need someone to help you reflect upon your actions, feelings, and perceptions.
- Examine district professional development offerings, and participate in all available opportunities that address areas in which you might be assessed as "basic" or "proficient" (see Figure 4.2).
- Contact school and/or district partners that might offer free or reduced rate professional development opportunities (i.e., higher education institutions or nonprofit organizations).

Figure 4.2 provides a simple guide to assist principals in assessing their professional learning needs. To use the guide, principals record every reform topic currently under way or in the pipeline for implementation.

Figure 4.2	Professional Learning Assessment Guide	
Transformation Topic	Self-Assessment (advanced, proficient, or basic)	Plan to Accelerate Professional Understanding

Then they assess their understanding of the reform effort. Principals who are "advanced" can fluidly describe the district initiative, they can integrate the transformation effort authentically into existing job-embedded structures, and they have the support staff in place to assist with this work. Principals who are "proficient" can describe the district initiative, they can integrate the initiative into existing job-embedded structures with some restructuring, and they have support staff that can be trained to assist with this work. Principals who are "basic" cannot describe the district initiative, they do not have the existing job-embedded structure in place (which means that one will need to be created), and they do not currently have the support staff to assist with this work. Principals are encouraged to use the strategic engagement considerations outlined previously to accelerate their professional learning.

THE PRINCIPAL OF A SUCCESSFUL SCHOOL IS NOT *JUST* THE INSTRUCTIONAL LEADER, BUT *ALSO* THE COORDINATOR OF TEACHERS AS INSTRUCTIONAL LEADERS FOR EQUITY

The idea of principal as an instructional leader for equity is complicated further when individuals who were previously stellar classroom teachers ascend to the principalship and then struggle with creating structures that help others to become great teachers as defined, in part, by students' achievements.

Principled Practices 1

1. Define what effective instruction (instruction that causes learning in each student) looks like.

2. Describe how to know when effective instruction for each student is taking place.

3. Explain how curriculum, instruction, and assessment come together in the classroom to meet each student's academic needs.

4. Communicate how individuals other than the principal engage in instructional leadership for equity. Describe the "who" and "how" of a school's instructional leadership for equity work.

5. Instructional leadership for equity can (and should) extend the formal observation and evaluation process; therefore, establish a specific structure for informal walkthrough observations, job-embedded professional development, and utilization of instructional resources.

6. Use resource acquisition and building maintenance to create ideal learning and teaching environments focused on equity.

The principalship requires a different skill set, which includes the ability to create the conditions for average teaching to evolve into good teaching and for good teaching to evolve into great teaching. This skill set also requires principals not only to create equitable teaching structures but also to maintain them in the midst of significant educational change. The question then becomes how principals become chief learners and chief change managers for equity while still assuming the role of chief instructional leaders for equity. Again, this is the leadership-for-equity dilemma that affects today's principals.

If we revisit Dodge's dilemma, it highlights the complexity of being chief learner and change manager for equity. Dodge was attempting to learn a new curriculum, implement a new teacher and administration evaluation system, and train a new assistant principal. At the same time, he was required to facilitate the new learning for his school community. Souba (2007) states that leadership inherently deals with change in that leaders must set vision during change, select the correct individuals to assist and lead the change, and then create the appropriate culture in which staff are supported and encouraged to do the "unknown or yet to be defined" work ahead. Dodge was unable to cope with the change and, therefore, was unable to serve as chief learner and chief change manager for equity.

As we examine this idea further, we recognize that today's principals are often charged with leading others even when new learning is new for them as well. Souba (2007) maintains that leaders respond to change "by more creating, often by embarking on a new strategic vision" that clarifies the direction and rationale for the change (p. 5). This is a powerful idea and is often, we believe, a significant challenge for many principals. Figure 4.3 identifies three vital change factors and essential behaviors for principals attempting to serve as both chief learner and chief change manager for equity.

Principled Practices 2

1. Intentionally schedule time during the work day to read, review, and record questions regarding new curricula, programs, and/or initiatives. All questions should be directed to the curricular leader, program director, and/or initiative contact person. Maintain and review a log of this activity weekly with the leadership team. Be deliberate with this work.

2. Identify three individuals (internal and/or external staff) to become your "think partners" regarding each new curriculum, program, and/or initiative. These individuals should be more knowledgeable than you. (You can always serve as a coach to others, but you must first commit to do the work yourself.)

3. The preceding two principled practices must be framed using an equity lens. The new curriculum, program, and/or initiative must be viewed from the context of who is being served well and who is not.

Figure 4.3   Considerations for a Chief Learner and Chief Change
Manager for Equity

Potential Change Factor	Chief Learner Behaviors for Equity	Chief Change Manager Behaviors for Equity
• Change in the deficit model of thinking regarding students (i.e., some students are broken and need to be repaired)	• Stay abreast of culturally responsive instructional processes and curriculum materials and resources that allow students to see themselves. Create competency regarding asset-based thinking to develop positive perspectives regarding each student.	• Deliberately use equity learning cycles, equity audits, students' voices, and student data (quantitative and qualitative) to readjust and center the work on areas that will eliminate achievement gaps. • Constantly frame the instructional equity conversations from an asset-based mindset, according to which each student has assets, and education should build on those assets to engage students actively in the teaching and learning process.
• Change in the curricula, programs, and/or initiatives	• Stay abreast of new curricula, programs, and/or initiatives that include multiple access and entry points for each student to experience success.	• Frame all new curricula, programs, and/or initiatives as new components of your instructional vision for equity. Introduce this work as a strategic shift in the instructional vision for equity to respond to the work ahead.
• Change in the communication plan used to roll out the curricula, programs, and/or initiatives	• If information is not readily available (meaning the curricula, programs, and/or initiatives are being written at the same time that implementation is expected), create learning teams that require key members of your leadership team to "own" various components of the learning.	• Frame the new information in the context of the desired change. Create opportunities for individuals to express their frustrations with the lack of information while concurrently establishing structures for those frustrations to evolve into creative solutions to address the lack of information. Creative solutions must be truly welcomed, encouraged, and even celebrated.

All of this might sound logical, or you might even think that this work sounds easy. Our experience, however, has been that it is extremely difficult to do this work. The principals we encounter in our day-to-day work are yearning for opportunities to make sense of it all. To that end, we are attempting to guide principals and district leaders who are focused on confronting and then addressing the leadership-for-equity dilemma.

PRINCIPAL ELIZABETH SPRINGFIELD: PRINCIPAL AS FACILITATOR OF EQUITY AND ACCESS FOR EACH STUDENT

Today we sometimes hear principals say, "We are all about equity and access in our school community," or "We create equitable conditions for all students to be successful," or perhaps "All means all in our school." These sentiments sound great, and they are almost always said in an authentic, caring fashion. Regrettably, student achievement data indicate that our sentiments have not, in general, yielded equitable student outcomes for all student groups. This is especially true for traditionally marginalized groups of students.

A review of classroom enrollment data in many public schools reveals that students of color, linguistically diverse students, and students living in poverty are overwhelming enrolled in lower-level courses, and they are often ill prepared to take higher-level, college preparatory courses. According to Ferguson (1991, 1998) and Kincheloe (2004, 2010), the causes for the disparity in performance include but are not limited to the following:

- Lowered expectations for students of color, linguistically diverse students, and students living in poverty
- Growing income inequality and lack of resources in low-income school districts
- Unequal access to experienced teachers
- An increased number of certified teachers instructing students of color in subjects outside their area of certification
- Unconscious and sometimes conscious bias by teachers and administrators
- School procedures designed to group students based on skills to accelerate students and promote prepared college and career-ready graduates; in many instances, however, the proclaimed goal of acceleration often is not met

These factors produce an opportunity gap and contribute to the longstanding achievement gap for students of color, linguistically diverse students, and students living in poverty (Ferguson, 1991, 1998). Additionally, principals are often challenged to identify and correct school practices within their control that serve to exacerbate opportunity and achievement gaps. To illustrate this point, let's consider Springfield's situation.

Like many other principals across the nation, Springfield reported disparities in outcomes based on student demographic data. Specifically, she identified her dilemma as follows: All African American, Hispanic, special education, and ELL students consistently scored below proficiency on quarterly benchmark assessments. Teachers were trying to meet students' needs, but the teachers kept saying, "We need more resources and interventions for these students." Springfield believes the underlying reason for student underachievement is that the teachers are not equipped with instructional toolkits to help them meet students' instructional needs. Therefore, she plans to collaborate with her school district's professional development office to provide a series of differentiated, job-embedded sessions combined with a book study on culturally responsive instruction. Springfield is attempting to support student achievement by professionally developing teachers. This is a good first step, right? Our immediate response is "Absolutely." However, there is a "but" that we must explore together. To engage in this exploration, please review the questions outlined below:

- Which teachers are instructing students of color, linguistically diverse students, and students living in poverty?
  - Are these teachers teaching in their area of certification?
  - Are these teachers new or experienced teachers?
  - Are these teachers regularly attending work?
  - Are these teachers using cultural competency to frame their work?
- What course sequence is being offered to students?
  - Were there any years when the students were not engaged in a high-quality core instructional program?
- Are there gaps in the instructional schedule that might account for students' lack of skill attainment (absences, suspensions, and/or mobility factors)?
- Are there data (using all available testing data) that suggest students of color, linguistically diverse students, and students living in poverty ever meet state standards?
  - Are there pockets of excellent performance within each identified student group, or are *all* identified students performing below grade-level expectations?
    - ❖ If there are pockets of excellence, explore further by reviewing student cumulative records, talking to staff, and conversing with students.

These questions are intended to serve as probes. Springfield and other principals confronted by similar circumstances should reflect on these questions and attempt to answer them prior to determining the appropriate next steps. Accordingly, Springfield's experience highlights the third component of the leadership dilemma: principal as a facilitator of equity and access for each student.

The idea of educational equity has been long debated and discussed; however, few sources move beyond simply defining the concept (Bitters, 1999). That is why we developed our three-pronged Data-Driven Student-Centered Framework for Achieving Educational Equity, which we introduced in Chapter 1 and revisit here (see Figure 4.4). According to this framework, our definition of *educational equity* focuses on student outcomes. The instructional leader uses the three central prongs to describe the school's or district's context for equity work: descriptions of achievement gaps, of learners, and of progress toward high standards for each student. We invite you to adopt this definition if your school district and/or school community does not have an operational definition of educational equity. Once you are clear about your operational definition of educational equity, we then challenge you to be extremely transparent regarding how educational equity is defined in your district and/or school community. We further urge you to serve as an ambassador for this definition (a) by clearly communicating the definition through words (print and spoken) to all stakeholders and (b) by creating internal structures, processes, and protocols to guide your daily thinking and leadership relative to educational equity.

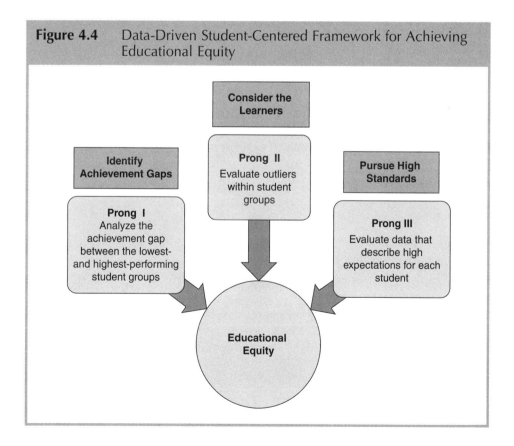

Figure 4.4   Data-Driven Student-Centered Framework for Achieving Educational Equity

Figure 4.5 Educational Equity Thinking Structure		
Educational Equity Prong I: Identify Achievement Gaps	**Educational Equity Prong II: Consider the Learners**	**Educational Equity Prong III: Pursue High Standards**
• Are all teachers striving for 100 percent of every student in each student group to meet grade-level expectations?	• Do you examine gaps between and among students in the same student group?	• Does each student in your school community have access to the core curriculum every day? What checks and balances are in place to ensure that each student has high-quality teachers?
• Are culturally responsive teaching practices being used to promote high achievement for each student?	• Do you seek to analyze underperformance trends within the same student group (e.g., by speaking to specific students, analyzing cumulative folders, speaking to former teachers, conversing with parents)? Do you adjust practice based on your findings?	• Does each student have access to rigorous courses? • Is there equal access to rigorous courses? • Are rigorous courses encouraged and supported for each student?
• How frequently are you using data to progress monitor, adjust instruction, and then progress monitor again to ensure that each student is meeting the same high standards?	• Do you analyze school procedures, policies, and practices that may contribute to some students performing better than other students (applicable for all three prongs of the educational equity definition)?	• What supports are in place to ensure that students accessing rigorous courses will likely be successful?
• Is there an aligned written, taught, and assessed curriculum that takes into account teacher capacity and students' identities? How are common assessments used to promote high student achievement for each student?	• Is there an aligned written, taught, and assessed curriculum that takes into account teacher capacity and students' identities? How are common assessments used to promote high student achievement for each student?	• Is there an aligned written, taught, and assessed curriculum that takes into account teacher capacity and students' identities? How are common assessments used to promote high student achievement for each student?
• How do you capture and then use students' voices in progress monitoring this work?	• How do you capture and then use students' voices in progress monitoring this work?	• How do you capture and then use students' voices in progress monitoring this work?

> **Principled Practices 3**
>
> 1. Disrupt status quo thinking by asking specific questions associated with each prong of the educational equity definition (see Figure 4.5 for some initial questions).
>
> 2. Be comfortable with being uncomfortable. Equity is a concept that may not be embraced by all initially (including you, and it is okay—just do not stay in that space). Use clear and easily understandable data to help explain why we cannot wait to adjust practice when the expectation is that each student will be successful *now*.
>
> 3. Share individual students' and teachers' personal narratives. Put a face to this work. We often become inspired and then motivated when we hear success stories.

Principals new to this work may refer to Figure 4.5 for a structure that can be used to guide their thinking about educational equity.

What happens when you start to facilitate the conversation using an educational equity lens? What happens when you better understand the "why" behind the opportunity and achievement gaps? What happens when you try to address the "why" and teachers, staff, and parents question your leadership? What happens when others do not see the need to change practices to ensure that each student achieves high academic success? These questions will likely emerge when you start facilitating for equity and access for each student. However, these questions are absolutely essential to your evolution as a facilitator for equity and access for each student. As with all new ways of thinking and/or acting, you will need to ascertain the appropriate entry point for this work within your school community. For us, the appropriate entry point is simple. Use Prong I, and clearly and frequently communicate to your school community that your data—not local, state, or federal data—dictate that using an equity and access lens is the only way to begin to address the opportunity and achievement gaps. You would still include all local, state, and federal accountability structures requiring the reduction of achievement gaps, but you will not change outcomes for students by simply doing what you have always done!

CONCLUSION

We began this chapter with three principals' narratives. Their reflections at a summer leadership retreat served as the backdrop for our exploration of the concept we describe as the leadership-for-equity dilemma.

Throughout this chapter, we have attempted to introduce and then explain the three components of this dilemma:

1. Principal as an instructional leader for equity;

2. Principal as a chief learner and change manager for equity; and

3. Principal as facilitator of equity and access for each student.

We offer you guidance on confronting and then directly addressing the leadership-for-equity dilemma. Although challenging and, at times, uncomfortable, this work is necessary if we want to give each student access to a quality instructional program every single day in every public school setting. To achieve this end, we invite principals to reflect on this discussion in relation to the PACE Framework. The PACE Framework is designed to assist principals in defying persistent and lingering opportunity and achievement gaps. Still, principals must bring to PACE a "choose to be great" mindset, which can be achieved by intentionally analyzing their leadership development through the three interrelated components of the leadership-for-equity dilemma.

Principled Practices Summary

1. Instructional leaders should fully understand the components of the leadership dilemma: (a) principal as an instructional leader for equity, (b) principal as a chief learner and change manager for equity, and (c) principal as a facilitator of equity and access for each student.

2. Instructional leaders must juxtapose their skills with the components of the leadership-for-equity dilemma in order to gain a true assessment of the "self-work" ahead.

3. Instructional leaders cannot simply talk about equity and access without a self-examination of their leadership, school culture, and students' achievement data.

4. Principals attempting to transform their school communities aim to *eliminate* the achievement gap and not simply close it; therefore, an intentional equity agenda is not just needed—it is essential.

DISCUSSION QUESTIONS AND ACTIVITIES

1. Identify the level of change in your school district.
   a. List the new initiatives and programs in your district.
   b. List the district leaders of those initiatives and programs.

2. Assess which components of the leadership-for-equity dilemma are areas of strength for you and which are areas of growth opportunity.
   a. Are there any practices you can start embracing immediately to decrease the impact of the leadership-for-equity dilemma?
   b. Are there any practices you will need to phase in because implementation will require additional resources before you begin?
   c. What internal resources are available to assist you in addressing the leadership-for-equity dilemma?
   d. What external resources are available to assist you in addressing the leadership-for-equity dilemma?

3. Identify a small group of professionals with whom you can begin to plan strategically to discuss the leadership-for-equity dilemma. As a collective group, identify group activities to help address the overall leadership-for-equity dilemma:
   a. For example, consider taking turns shadowing each other and taking notes on all activities.
   b. Then go back and code each activity as directly linked to instructional leadership for equity. Ask yourself, what professional learning do I need in this area?
   c. Share your finding with the individual shadowed. Use this as an opportunity to recalibrate.

4. Conduct a self-audit of your leadership-for-equity work. On any given day, review your calendar to identify if what you are doing is linked to improving student achievement using an equity and access lens for each student. Repeat activity 3b as an independent and reflective activity.

5

Taking Instructional Leadership for Equity Into the Classroom

The Daily Quality Instruction Challenge

It is teaching that must be improved to push us along the path to success.

(Stigler & Hiebert, 1999)

In Chapter 4 we described the dilemma of leading for equity using three ideas critical to moving a school toward transformation. The importance of principal as instructional leader for equity, principal as chief learner and change manager for equity, and principal as facilitator of equity and access for each student is foundational in transforming a school or system. In this chapter we delve deeper into an examination of what it looks like when instructional leadership with an equity lens is taken into the classroom. This book is premised on the idea that, to eliminate gaps in achievement and outcomes, students must have access to quality instruction every day. Furthermore, the assessment of access to quality instruction needs to happen in the context of educational equity. This is critical because we contend, as do Stigler and Hiebert (1999), that teaching and learning must improve if our schools are to achieve high outcomes for each student. The instructional process is complex. Leaders can observe many different elements in a classroom. In this chapter we explore the most important fundamentals when the goal is to dislodge patterns of underservice to diverse students. We focus on three conditions critical to student learning: active engagement, relevant learning experiences, and use of data to monitor students' regular access to these conditions.

Why these three conditions? Far too often in schools serving marginalized populations, you can find students' heads down on their desks, students being sent out of the classroom for misbehavior, or students demonstrating compliant behavior with little depth in knowledge. However, meeting high achievement outcomes for each student cannot occur in learning environments in which these are acceptable conditions. We believe that instructional leadership for equity must make its way into the classroom as the first and most powerful demonstration of a school's commitment to putting students' learning first. A student interviewed in the book *Fires in the Bathroom: Advice for Teachers from High School Students* expresses the feelings of many students: "Camilla [a student] told me that they weren't going in because that teacher 'didn't know how to teach,' and just kept wasting their time" (Cushman & Delpit, 2003, p. xvii). Camilla's comments are clearly those of a student who does not feel valued, and her statement raises a key question: How can we possibly eliminate gaps in achievement and raise standards for each student if the instruction—the teaching and learning—is viewed as just a waste of time? Further, what happens in a classroom that makes young people feel their time is being wasted? Finally, what must we do about it? The short response to all of these questions is that instruction cannot be deemed "quality instruction" if young people are disengaged and feel ignored during the learning experience. Thus begins our examination of the key leadership behaviors that support access to quality instruction for each learner.

QUALITY INSTRUCTIONAL OPPORTUNITIES ARE AN EQUITY IMPERATIVE

The importance of quality teaching for each student cannot be overstated for leaders pursuing educational equity. According to Jerald, Haycock, and Wilkens (2009), "Classroom teachers have a far bigger impact on student achievement than any other factor in education, an impact that literally can make or break a student's chances for success" (p. 1). What we sometimes miss, however, is that quality teaching cannot exist if its companion—deep learning—isn't present. To uncouple teaching and learning is to miss the mark in pursuing educational equity. For this reason, the PACE Framework begins with the leader's vision of quality instruction that is premised on student learning (see Chapter 3). Bold instructional leadership is a necessary condition to support schoolwide quality teaching and learning practices. Leaders need to be clear about the vision that will guide the assessment of students' access to daily quality instruction. When this picture is clear in the leader's mind, the work with the team (leadership, teachers, students, and parents) can begin productively.

The competing demands of testing accountability, curriculum implementation requirements, and supervisors' expectations are very real issues that principals manage on a daily basis. However, these issues of the immediate must not undermine that which is most important, ensuring that students are afforded a learning experience that moves them every day closer to full preparation for the rigors of life in the twenty-first century. What this means is that principals must show up in the school, in the central office, and in the superintendent's office as instructional leaders pursuing an equity agenda. This focus on learning is a choice—a clearly articulated choice that must be made when leading for equity. Instructional leaders pursuing equity create space and opportunity for teachers to thrive professionally. In a school or system serving a diverse student population, professional growth should be evaluated based on one's ability to facilitate the academic growth of each student group. This is the foundation for institutionalization of the practice and culture needed for school transformation. As we move into this chapter, take a few minutes to complete with your leadership team the self-assessment in Figure 5.1. The outcome of this assessment will illuminate the connections between your definition of instructional leadership and the tenets we use to move instructional leadership for equity into the classroom. Your leadership team should actively discuss and examine any differences found between their daily practice and the equity-based instructional leadership practice outlined here. The results of this assessment will likely expand your school's ability to bring about high academic outcomes for each student.

When you begin to apply questions of equity and access to daily teaching and learning practice, you are sure to identify habits (school and individual ones) that are marginalizing to some learners and need to change. For many, change creates discomfort. Pursuing an equity agenda in the field means that you are asking your staff (as you challenge yourself) to move from practices that they know well to practices about which they may be less knowledgeable or in which they have less competency.

Figure 5.1   Self-Assessment of Readiness to Take Equity-Based Instructional Leadership Into the Classroom

1. Instructional leaders are chief learners and change managers who use an equity framework.
   a. Name the last *new* professional learning opportunity you experienced that was prompted by your use of an equity lens in defining a situation.

   b. Describe actions you took to build your own capacity to understand the situation. (Include any collaborative efforts.)

   c. Describe the process you used to engage others in solution seeking. What is the evidence the process worked or is working?

2. Instructional leaders confront adaptive challenges (challenges that do not present simple or known solutions).
   a. Describe an adaptive challenge with which you have engaged your school community.

   b. Describe the process you have used or are using to engage your staff.

   c. In what ways are you positioned to assess your team's progress?

3. Instructional leaders use strategic plans with structures for accountability.
   a. Does your school have a strategic plan?

   b. Does the plan explicitly address your equity challenges?

   c. How are you benchmarking progress?

   d. What is the communication plan?

4. Instructional leaders are courageous, deliberate, and committed.
   a. What opposition have you experienced in your adaptive work?

   b. How are you managing opposition?

   c. How are you galvanizing support?

   d. How are you maximizing effective communication and inclusion of multiple perspectives?

   Use the results of these reflections to discuss your individual and team readiness to apply an equity lens to the teaching and learning process.

When you consider daily quality instruction, you are asking your staff to engage consistently in this new way of being because it represents the means for meeting the needs of each learner. Because disequilibrium is a part of the change process, as you prepare to take your equity agenda into your interactions with teachers and students, assessing your leadership team and your teachers' readiness for the adaptive process is critical. Your leadership team should have an honest sense of its personal and professional commitment on the items outlined in Figure 5.1. The goal is to create a school environment in which access to quality instruction for each student is the norm and demographically predictable achievement trends are the anomaly. Constant awareness of this goal is critical for ensuring that your leadership team can provide the kind of expert feedback and capacity-building support that teachers need to grow and develop into leaders of learning for each student. Principals cannot be on the instructional sidelines in schools that are pursuing educational equity. In fact, education can serve as the engine for social mobility for underserved students, but school leaders have to conduct the train.

Instructional leaders who are chief learners and change managers for equity and who desire to ensure access to quality instruction for each student need to take three key actions in order to move instructional leadership for equity into the classroom:

1. Acting on the imperative that each learner is engaged

2. Insisting on purposeful, relevant teaching and learning as a norm

3. Acting on data in making decisions about the learning program

The order of the key actions is not meant to signify importance or sequence; rather, these actions constitute nonnegotiable behaviors if the goal is to eliminate disparities in student achievement. In the field of education, a robust body of literature supports the importance of student engagement, relevant learning, and the use of data (Bambrick-Santoyo, 2010; Bellanca & Rodriguez, 2007; Boudett & Steele, 2007; Boykin & Noguera, 2011; Johnson, 2002; Johnson & LaSalle, 2010; Kelley & Shaw, 2009; Ladson-Billings, 1995, 2009; Lemov, 2010; Tatum, 2005). We argue that the aspects of the complex teaching and learning transaction most critical to eliminating gaps are (a) the use of the PACE Framework and (b) maintenance of a consistent focus on every learner. In schools and districts actively pursuing global competitiveness for each learner, these efforts are being supported by action and ongoing evaluation. In the sections that follow, we unpack the three key actions using the lens of a diverse student population as the frame of reference.

KEY ACTION 1: INSTRUCTIONAL LEADERS FOR EQUITY FOCUS ON EVERY LEARNER BEING ENGAGED

Active engagement is an essential condition for learning. According to Boykin and Noguera (2011), "At the most fundamental level, to optimize learning, a teacher must ensure that students are engaged in the learning process" (p. 42). They also suggest that meaningful engagement for students from diverse backgrounds has a greater impact on achievement than does instruction. The process of engaging students in deep meaningful learning is a part of what it means to *provide quality instruction.* Leaders need to ensure that four underlying conditions are in place in order to support teacher practice that engages every learner:

1. Values are assessed by behaviors.

2. Operative cultural competence is a condition of engagement.

3. Cultural competence is used as instructional practice.

4. Cultural competence is observable.

These conditions are described in detail later in this chapter.

Teachers select learning resources and activities, among many other things. These choices heavily influence student engagement. Key Action 1 says that instructional leaders leading for equity immerse themselves in both the process and the evaluation of how such decisions unfold for the instructional staff. Moving leadership for equity into the classroom means that classroom visits and observations are done with a specific lens on engagement. For instructional leaders to commit to this key action, they must first deliberately address many unexamined assumptions. Figure 5.2 outlines six critical assumptions that warrant examination as leaders work to ensure that each learner is engaged.

Figure 5.2   Reflective Activity: Six Critical Assumptions

As you collaborate with your leadership team, go on a walkthrough of your school or district, and assess how consistently you see evidence of the following:

1. Teachers believe in the potential of each student.
2. Teachers have high expectations for each student.
3. Teachers create conditions for each student to achieve the high expectations set.
4. Teachers do not have limiting perceptions about children that are based on stereotypes or personal biases.
5. Teachers create multiple opportunities for students to access content and/or skills.
6. Teachers create multiple opportunities for students to demonstrate acceptable ways of knowing.

To illustrate how to move the principal's (and the leadership team's) instructional leadership into the classroom, we examine the situation in one elementary school. Joyce Lane was a third-year leader who was starting the year in a new elementary school of about 500 students. The population was majority students of color (African American) and majority socioeconomically disadvantaged. About midway into the year, one of Lane's staff, a fourth-grade teacher, sent Lane an email about being afraid for her safety because she had kept four fourth-grade African American boys after school the day before and the way they "looked at her" made her uncomfortable. Lane engaged the teacher, who happened to be white and female, as are most elementary school teachers across the nation, and asked her to describe what was happening that was causing her discomfort. Lane also asked about the teacher's beliefs about these particular children. The teacher offered that this was her first "urban experience" and the students seemed menacing to her. She didn't have language to assign to specific behaviors, but she kept recounting how the students made her feel.

People working in education across the country have the same kinds of "feelings" that the fourth-grade teacher described. Lane can develop the best school plans, academic programs, and intervention supports available, but if the staff share this fourth-grade teacher's feelings, students' access to quality instruction will be compromised. This is a reality that instructional leaders pursuing educational equity cannot avoid. As the year progressed, Lane continued to engage and coach the fourth-grade teacher, challenging some of her perceptions of students' behavior by discussing the various cultural contexts that contribute to different interpretations. In the end, however, the teacher chose to leave the school. She indicated that this situation was not what she had signed up for when she decided to become a teacher. Lane understood and shared that embracing each student attending the school was the only way staff would be successful at that elementary school.

As they advance their equity work, leaders need to be well acquainted with the truth of the six critical assumptions on their campuses. We start with these assumptions because they constitute a part of the invisible, unexamined culture in school contexts. Since these assumptions are stated but only infrequently examined empirically, we want you to pause and reflect as you consider them. Can you demonstrate that these assumptions are true about the staff members leading children in your building? If, in your reflection, you have questions about a staff member or some aspect of your overall school culture, don't dismiss it. Begin the work of your equity-focused instructional leadership right at the point of your concern. All of the other key actions, conditions, and principles that follow in this chapter rely on the six critical assumptions as their foundation. If a deep, abiding "do whatever is necessary" attitude is not collectively present, then you will not be able to interrupt disparities in achievement.

Putting First That Which Should Be First: Values Are Assessed by Behaviors

Moving instructional leadership into the classroom requires a consistent focus on issues that are largely underestimated and underexamined, for example, what it takes to fashion learning that ignites the interests of varied student groups. Also, the current transition in public education to the Common Core State Standards is moving assessments of learning from pen and paper to the virtual arena, which creates greater opportunities for student engagement. Although there is increased opportunity as we expand the means of engagement, the fundamental question of what engages each student is not answered if the question is not addressed through the lens of the students we serve in our schools today. The challenge is to disrupt the marginalization of underserved populations by structuring the educational process responsively. Leaders focused on meeting the needs of each student cannot leave the answers to these critical questions to chance, to the luck of assignment to an effective teacher. Instructional leaders leading for equity must have a deliberate focus on engagement.

Think about the experience of Principal Lane. Do you really believe that quality academic engagement was happening on a daily basis for students in the fourth-grade class with the fearful teacher? Regardless of the instructional method by which we expect learning to occur, for students who are underperforming, a high-quality, engaging experience is a necessary condition if trends of disparate achievement are to be interrupted.

Principled Practices 1

1. Challenge any use of instructional time that does not include cognitive, affective, and behavioral engagement.

2. Assess engagement through conversations with students that include discourse on the reflective process they use in learning.

3. Deliberately look for evidence of the use of cultural knowledge in engagement practices.

In putting first things first, leaders committed to equity don't look beyond teachers like the one from Lane's school. What do equity-focused instructional leaders do to create conditions to engage each learner? The first step is to envision teaching and learning explicitly through the capacity of staff to engage each learner. This means intentionally defining what cultural competence is and what role it serves in both student engagement and instructional practice.

Operative Cultural Competence Is a Condition of Engagement

According to the National Education Association (2013), "Cultural competence is having an awareness of one's own cultural identity and views about differences, and the ability to learn and build on the varying cultural and community norms of students and their families." We are all cultural beings—each of us. We make sense of the world through a lens that is defined by our lived and learned experiences. No one is a blank slate, and the entry points to learning are varied. Schools, and by extension learning, cannot be divorced from a cultural context. Learning to operate in the presence of differences is the hallmark of responsive instruction. As a consequence, equity-focused instructional leadership practice should emerge from the assessment of our individual and collective demonstrations of cultural competence.

More specifically, as we understand how our cultural identity influences how we lead schools, we can create conditions that allow teachers to see how their cultural identities influence how they lead classrooms. We need teachers to create learning opportunities in this way. Specifically, how is knowledge of students' lived experiences informing how teachers seek to engage them (Ladson-Billings, 1995, 2009)? These ideas may seem intuitive, but leaders need to give permission for cultural considerations to be a priority in the classroom. In the cultural context, the questions of affective engagement (how students feel about the learning), behavioral engagement (what students do to learn), and cognitive engagement (how students intellectually comprehend) can be examined in a manner that allows the influence of multiple perspectives. The validation of multiple perspectives increases access to the learning environment. The example that follows illustrates how self-assessment of cultural competence shapes leadership that promotes engaging each student.

Joan Green was in her tenth year at a large urban high school serving nearly 1,200 students, most of whom were African American. In the spring of 2012, several of her students expressed an interest in leading a showing of support for the family of Trayvon Martin, an unarmed seventeen-year-old

African American male who had been killed in Sanford, Florida, by neighborhood watchman George Zimmerman. The students told Green that they wanted to wear hoodies (which Trayvon had been wearing at the time of his murder) to school as a show of solidarity with Trayvon's family. Green had some concern, since hoodies were not in compliance with the dress code, but she agreed to let the students wear the hoodies as long as they went to class and did not cause any disruptions. Several teachers heard about the approval Green had granted the students, and they contacted the teachers' union. Their position was that Trayvon Martin had not been a good example and that the school should not support the students in any effort to show support for this young man's family. The union contacted Green and made her aware of the teachers' opposition. She decided that she would allow the students to wear the hoodies for one day, but there would be no other action or discussion of the incident.

In conferring with Green about this incident, we made two readily apparent observations: (a) the normative climate in the school was one in which multiple perspectives were not being recognized or acknowledged, and (b) teachers did not typically consider the interests and passions of their students when making teaching and learning decisions. These types of situations, in which students are interested in things that adults are not and adults use power to create limits that are exclusive, are too common in schools serving diverse populations. The most counterintuitive consequence of such decisions is that they are antithetical to whole-school active engagement.

Cultural Competence Is Used as Instructional Practice

Twenty-first-century instructional leadership is all about transforming twentieth-century teaching and learning in a manner that positions teachers to be effective facilitators of students' learning. Teachers who believe that it is unimportant to know and engage with the conditions and factors shaping the prism through which young people come to understand the world cannot engage them effectively. For example, the rise in accessibility and affordability of cell phones has expanded access to cell phones for many families. Young people use this technology at earlier and earlier ages. The shorthand text language is an efficient means of communicating; therefore, many people—young and old—use it. Knowledge of text language can be used as a tool to engage and scaffold students' development of written language, among other things. Teachers need to recognize such cultural assets and leaders need to support the identification of these types of socialized learning experiences as essential to the learning environment. In other words, teachers need to use cultural capital as an instructional practice. More specifically, they need to use cultural capital as an engagement strategy (Ladson-Billings, 1995). The idea here is that lived experiences are a form of capital that has instructional value. Just as socialization is happening in the lives of white, middle- and upper-class students, it is happening for our students of color, students with economic challenges, and students receiving special education services. In short, each student comes to school with a cultural reference point shaped by socialization. Culturally competent leaders acknowledge and demonstrate the value of their students' lived experiences through the influences these experiences have on school practices, especially inside the classroom. Effective equity-based instructional leadership cannot possibly be offered outside of a context of cultural competence.

Let's take a look at another example of how cultural competence can be used as instructional practice. Reconsider Principal Green's situation. What if more time had been spent in discussion with the students who wanted to support Trayvon Martin's family? What if Green had taken the time to find out what was motivating students' interest? What if she had asked the students to meet with a group of teachers to share their thoughts so that the community would better understand their thoughts and feelings? What if she had probed what the teachers meant when they said that Trayvon wasn't a "good example"? What if Green had helped to make the connection between how the students and teachers were experiencing the incident while identifying the differences and similarities to enhance communication? The answers to these "what if" questions illustrate how we convert cultural competence from simply an idea into a practice. The critical understanding for equity-focused leaders is that this type of instructional practice should not just occur during certain times of the year or in celebration of some event, but rather, daily instruction should begin with that which has students actively making sense of their world (Ladson-Billings, 1995).

Cultural Competence Is Observable

Cultural competence is often asserted but less often observed in teaching and learning. Additionally, cultural competence is often aspired to but rarely achieved in schools and organizations. Awareness is the foundation of competence in the day-to-day schooling process. Hence, Figure 5.3 offers a model for beginning to build cultural awareness in your school or organization. Why a model? Building cultural competence requires personal, interpersonal, professional, and organizational introspection and reflection. In short, you must commit to seeing and understanding your personal cultural dispositions and the cultural dispositions of others in the school community.

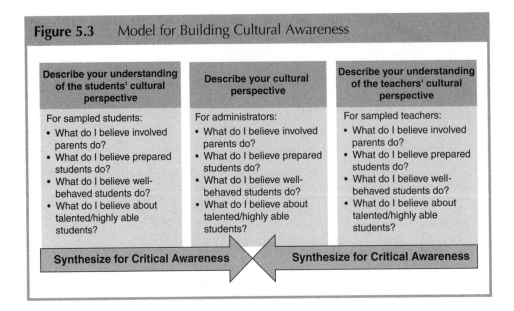

Figure 5.3   Model for Building Cultural Awareness

Describe your understanding of the students' cultural perspective	Describe your cultural perspective	Describe your understanding of the teachers' cultural perspective
For sampled students: • What do I believe involved parents do? • What do I believe prepared students do? • What do I believe well-behaved students do? • What do I believe about talented/highly able students?	For administrators: • What do I believe involved parents do? • What do I believe prepared students do? • What do I believe well-behaved students do? • What do I believe about talented/highly able students?	For sampled teachers: • What do I believe involved parents do? • What do I believe prepared students do? • What do I believe well-behaved students do? • What do I believe about talented/highly able students?
Synthesize for Critical Awareness		**Synthesize for Critical Awareness**

This knowledge building needs to follow a process. The model provides a simple mechanism to enable educators to begin this exploration. For cultural competence to become practice, educators must make direct efforts to gain cultural knowledge. In gaining this knowledge, educators need to be able to discuss stereotypes, biases, and individual perceptions. Leaders could use this model to begin the conversation that leads to the acquisition of cultural knowledge. Education leaders must be aware that their perceptions of the lived experiences of others is not always accurate. If our beliefs are rooted in biases or stereotypes, then we need to be the first to demonstrate our commitment to the value of all children. Equity-focused principals build cultural competence on a personal level, which shows up in their interactions with others and in their organizational leadership. The conversations these types of leaders have with staff are very different from those that leaders not doing their own intrapersonal cultural competence work have with their staffs. Principal Lane's engagement with the fourth-grade teacher resulted specifically from her own journey to becoming more culturally competent. As a consequence, she offered instructional leadership through that lens.

Interestingly, there are no situations in our lives in which culture is not at play. As adults in education, and leaders at that, we can use our power to create a culture that then becomes invisible to us. When we experience the cultural context for learning and engagement in schools serving traditionally marginalized populations, we typically see environments that are exclusionary. The data tell the story: lower academic achievement, higher suspension rates, and higher referral rates for excluded learning environments. These trends do not tell the story of an inclusive learning environment. The challenge for leaders pursuing educational equity is that they need to understand the story of exclusion that these trends tell.

The three-part model illustrated in Figure 5.3 is designed to assist members of a school community in gathering information about self, teachers, and students to build the foundation for culturally competent instructional practice. This model can be modified to include other stakeholders such as parents and community members. It should be used collaboratively to illustrate different perspectives, even as a school community "lives" the same experience. The feedback gathered in answering the questions in the model should be used to co-create an understanding of the elements needed for cultural competence in the school community. By extension, the information should also be used to develop instructional practices and procedures in the school. Because culture is always changing, use of the model should not be seen as a one-shot activity but as a recursive means of concretely addressing the necessity of building cultural competence by raising awareness.

Students, staff, and administrators can be randomly selected and surveyed when using this model. The goal is to get a working picture of the frame of reference for each group in a school. Responses to the questions in each section will give you a snapshot of the thinking that exists in your community about behavior and discipline, parent involvement, and academic achievement. Used with other data collection tools offered in this book, this model provides leaders additional information for understanding the culture in the building. This kind of understanding is critical for collaborating with others to decide how the culture needs to shift to meet the needs of each learner. As you define and refine your school vision using an equity lens, information from these types of analyses will help to deepen the practical implications of culturally responsive practice.

KEY ACTION 2: INSTRUCTIONAL LEADERS INSIST ON PURPOSEFUL, RELEVANT TEACHING AND LEARNING AS A DAILY NORM

In his book *Drive: The Surprising Truth About What Motivates Us,* Daniel Pink (1995) defines motivation as a function of three factors: autonomy, mastery, and purpose. In a departure from the conventional wisdom we use in education, in which motivation is described as a series of carrots and sticks, punishments and rewards, and/or positive and negative reinforcement practices, Pink offers that what motivates human beings is much more soulful. For Pink, motivating people in deep engagement means, in part, attending directly to the purpose motive. In other words, people need a sense of purposeful relevance to be truly motivated (Pink, 1995).

This brings us to Key Action 2, insisting on purposeful, relevant teaching and learning as a norm in the schooling process. Purpose and relevance are the companions of deep, meaningful engagement. The equity-focused instructional leader has to set the expectation that the learning environment must shift to create both a relevant and a purposeful learning experience for students—always. The challenge in making this climate shift is the modern reality that teachers feel pressed to "cover the curriculum" and "prepare students for tests." These worries overwhelm the central premise that schools exist to educate students, not to cover the curriculum or prepare for tests. The challenge related to Key Action 2 is to dismantle practices that interfere with teachers' ability to use the curriculum, technology, and assessments as tools that support relevant teaching and learning. Three foundational conditions undergird leaders' abilities to adaptively transform instructional practice toward relevant teaching and learning:

1. Expand the teaching purpose—live in the "why"

2. Begin with the end in mind—always answer "why" first

3. Create conditions that allow "whys" to drive learning

Leaders who believe that all teaching and learning should be relevant show an abiding belief in the potential of each young person and staff member. Instructional leaders are responsible for setting that tone and practice. We define quality instruction as practices that result in the deep, meaningful engagement of students as its most prominent feature.

Principled Practices 2

1. Collaborate to create a vision of relevant instruction that places the students at the center and identifies the curriculum as a resource to support each student's learning.

2. Inspect the outcomes of learning experiences both in conversation with students and via training produced. Use your assessments as data to determine work related to ensuring relevant learning opportunities.

3. Ensure that all training provided to staff is relevant to students' learning needs first. Use the data to demonstrate the connections between teacher training and students' learning.

This is achieved by actively dealing with the question: Relevant for whom? Although the goal is relevant learning experiences for each student, the process starts with instructional leaders' commitment to making the work required of staff relevant for their own professional practice. In leading for equity, one of the most powerful models we offer staff is related to the types of demands we make on their time. Therefore, we must ensure that our leadership prioritizes experiences that will enable teachers to make teaching and learning more relevant for children. This is an essential requisite in moving Key Action 2 into the classroom.

Evidence of relevant learning opportunities is assessed most easily by the products that students create, which are the most obvious manifestations of why the learning was important. If the "why" of learning is illustrated only by means of a test score, what do we truly know about what a child has learned? The "why" of learning is so critical to teaching and learning that it should be the question that teachers ask when they plan, the question that students answer, and the question that students use to move them through the process of learning. "Why" questions and answers are critical to rigorous cognitive engagement.

The instructional means that teachers use to engage students in relevant learning can run the gamut from direct instruction to teacher facilitation to teacher as academic guide, depending on the goal to be accomplished. To make decisions about instructional delivery and engagement, teachers practicing cultural competence will use knowledge of students, knowledge of the content to be learned, and knowledge of the best path to follow to get all students to the standard. Using our definition of quality instruction, one thing is clear: Teacher leadership and expertise is critical. Whereas teachers function as the leaders of students' learning every day, a critical question for instructional leaders is: Are my teachers actively conceptualizing their role in a manner that allows them to lead and guide students' learning in ways that demonstrate depth in learning? This question forms the backdrop for Key Action 2. Instructional leaders pursuing equity must insist on purposeful relevance in every lesson as a permanent condition in instructional practice.

Expand the Teaching Purpose—Live in the "Why"

Principal Jacobs spent the first few years of her principalship establishing relationships with local business and industry leaders, often having meetings with stakeholders to discuss the skills new workers were bringing to the job as well as those areas in which they were deficient. Jacobs also reached out to local colleges and universities to establish relationships with professors who taught primarily freshman-level courses in order to get their perspectives on the challenges that students contended with generally. Even though she was in charge of a middle school, Jacobs believed that the larger context of business and university was relevant to the training opportunities she would make accessible to her staff as the school worked to bridge gaps in students' regular access to quality instruction. Her behaviors were the kinds of actions taken by leaders who successfully respond to the needs of their student populations to ensure that the educational experience provided is as relevant and meaningful as possible.

The shift toward a focus on ensuring that each student graduates from high school ready for college or career is not without consequence. Those attempting to do a minor tweak here or there are missing the significant instructional gravity present in this moment. Core knowledge, social-emotional development, and new recognized literacies such as technological and entrepreneurial are all part of the relevance equation or what we call teaching in the "why." Although colleges and universities have a major role to play in ensuring that teacher preparation responds to these twenty-first-century learning demands, equity-focused instructional leaders build systems of support in their schools. The leader's ability to understand the school's teaching and learning dynamic is essential to build these systems. If teachers do not know the context for learning from the perspective of the students they teach, then their instructional leaders must provide relevant, job-embedded growth opportunities. Furthermore, embedding training in the context of the performance of the teaching and learning task is a way to support teachers efficiently while improving their professional skill level. The PACE Framework helps instructional leaders cogently build teacher capacity to provide consistently relevant learning experiences for each student (see Chapter 3).

Begin With the End in Mind—Always Answer the "Why" First

"Why do we have to learn this?" Unfortunately these words are heard far too often from young people in schools that need to improve. When they are spoken, we should hear what is really being said: "The learning about to take place will likely be superficial." Students who are underperforming need teaching and learning transactions to be deep and meaningful if they are to meet or exceed the standards. When we think of maximizing teacher-student transactions regularly in a quality instructional experience, we begin to see why we must insist on relevant learning experiences. The complication, though, is that too often we have unspoken expectations for our teachers about the central role of relevant learning experiences for students needing acceleration. As a result, teachers often rely too much on a given curriculum without considering whether the material is relevant to the student population being served.

Let's examine the way irrelevance plays out in teaching and learning when leaders don't insist that every learning experience occur in an environment in which teachers are answering the question "Why do students need to know this?" before students ask the question themselves. Let's revisit Principal Green's school for an example. Green and the district curriculum specialist went on a learning walk as a means of discussing the patterns each noticed over the course of a day. They walked into the class of a veteran language arts teacher who was engaging a group of seventh-grade students in a discussion of literary devices used in poetry. The class was identified as gifted and talented. There were few students of color in this class, especially boys of color. After quickly making that observation, the specialist began listening closely to the exchange between the teacher and students. The students were able to list the types of literary devices and examples of them. The teacher seemed pleased with the students' command of this information. Next, she gave the students lyrics from a song by the group R.E.M. and asked them to identify how the devices they discussed were exemplified in this song. This is when another, more subtle aspect of access began to emerge that was affecting the entire group. The young people had no background knowledge about R.E.M. They also had neither information on the context that shaped the message of the song nor any assistance in making connections between what they were reading and their own life experiences. What could have been an opportunity to move highly motivated, compliant youngsters deeply into learning turned into an assessment of learning at the level of demonstrated comprehension. The irony of the experience is that the students had already demonstrated comprehension at the beginning of the lesson. There was no need for those students to spend more time at that level of learning.

This example illustrates several critical points. First, transforming teaching and learning in a manner that places students first, while necessary for underserved students, also benefits the whole school population. In the case of this particular language arts teacher, the practice of beginning with what is relevant for the teacher was wasting instructional time for each student in that class. Second, the task of making teaching and learning relevant for students has varied dimensions. The lenses of race, class, and gender are obvious, but relevance also has generational (as illustrated in this example), social, and familial aspects. It is the cumulative effect of our lack of clarity on and command of the critical nature of answering the "why" question for young people that frustrates acceleration efforts. Furthermore and equally important, imagine the possibility presented when we systemically lead from a space that requires instruction to begin with the "why" rather than the "what." Teachers make a series of rapid decisions that are critically important to students. If teachers are not considering the continuum of situational variables that create relevance for students, then their positioning to lead learning in ways that are deep and meaningful is questionable.

Create Conditions That Allow the "Whys" to Drive the Learning

Instructional leaders focused on achieving equitable outcomes need to create structures that support the daily routine of establishing relevance in all learning situations. This should include learning that happens incidentally. The template shown in Figure 5.4 can be used to establish routines of instructional practice that begin by answering the "why" question. This template was designed specifically to equip school leaders to establish relevant learning as daily practice.

The template in Figure 5.4 is designed to identify the essential learning standards and daily objectives while connecting the learning for the day to past learning and future learning. The template also prompts teachers to contemplate how they will deliberately ensure students make meaningful connections with the learning. The point of the template is that relevant learning should be deliberately built in to instructional planning. It should not be left to last-minute, off-the-cuff thinking. Rather, it should be a planned learning experience skillfully guided by an educator who understands the learning context in which his or her students are operating. These prompts can be added into existing equity-focused learning tools to place an emphasis on relevant learning experiences.

These are the kinds of considerations that equity-focused instructional leaders should look for when they talk with students. The learning-walk protocol can be long and overwhelming. In a transformed school, the most important feedback that comes from visiting classrooms is the information you get from students. Because this feedback is critically important, it should be used to shape the guidance and support you offer to your staff. When students say things like "I don't know why we are learning this" or "We are learning this because it will help us to create," it serves as a powerful window into their journey into the learning. Professional development offerings based of this kind of feedback should be organized so that the instructional implications are very relevant to the adults. This is the type of modeling that equity-focused instructional leaders demonstrate in the practice of transforming a school culture.

A major barrier in our collective pursuit of high achievement outcomes for each student is the fact that we too often miss the big impact of little things.

| Figure 5.4 | Template for Creating Relevant Instructional Routines |

Lesson plan title:

Overarching standard:

Learning objective:

Student success criteria:

Why is this learning important?

- What past learning does it connect to?

- What future learning will it enhance?

- I will ensure students make these connections by . . .

- I am noticing my students make sense of what they are learning by . . .

If your staff is asking, "Why do we need to know this?" during professional development, you are missing an opportunity to model the behaviors you expect and move the imperative of relevant, purposeful learning into the classroom. Professional development experiences should be created expressly to provide staff with valuable, relevant training that will help them to meet the learning needs of each student.

KEY ACTION 3: INSTRUCTIONAL LEADERS ACT ON DATA IN MAKING DECISIONS ABOUT TEACHING AND LEARNING

According to Johnson and LaSalle (2010), "Data refers to information that can be used to describe conditions in schools and districts that affect students' school experiences in either positive or negative ways" (p. 195). Using this definition, we ask school leaders to begin thinking about the ways in which the term *data* can be expanded in their school or organization. The consequence of the high-stakes accountability to which we have become accustomed in public education is that when the word *data* is used, we immediately think of large-scale assessments, benchmarks, SAT data, Advanced Placement (AP) scores, and the like. These data are important and useful in understanding the function of our schools and school districts; however, data that can be used in the pursuit of educational equity are much broader in scope than those associated with large-scale standardized assessments. Key Action 3, which involves acting on data to make decisions about teaching and learning, requires a transformation in the way that data are used in teaching and learning. For us, this means three conditions are systematically in place:

1. Data are used in a manner that allows everyone to see themselves in the equity work.

2. Data are used appropriately in daily practice.

3. Data sources expand over time.

We make these assertions because in order to eliminate gaps in outcomes, we must eliminate gaps in access. Large-scale data, in isolation from other school-level data, will not position us to lead for educational equity. In the remainder of this section, we describe the three conditions using typical experiences in the daily work in public schools.

Using Johnson and LaSalle's definition, we submit that data are also information that describes students' access to quality learning opportunities.

Principled Practices 3

1. Establish the data context of the work of your school or organization. Staff members need to be able to demonstrate a practical understanding of what their roles are in eliminating unwanted patterns in student achievement.

2. Expand the types of data that are used to show achievement gaps as access gaps.

3. Systemize the use of a range of data so that it becomes a natural part of the work of every member of the school or organization.

We cannot systemically (within an entire school or district) lead for equity without using data that describe access. This way of thinking about data represents a cultural shift that must make its way throughout the organization in order for instructional leaders to lead for equity.

Use Data in a Manner That Allows Everyone to See Themselves in the Equity Work

It is 8:00 a.m. on the day before we begin a new school year in a mid-sized high school serving about 600 students, most of whom are students of color. The school has had years of challenge in improving the academic performance of its overall community. Over the past few years, the school has been on the state's "needs improvement" list, but at present it is identified only as a school district priority. The sentiment among the staff is that the difference in designation has only meant less scrutiny from outsiders. The graduation rate, average SAT scores, median class grade point average (GPA), and AP pass rates have all been well below district averages. The school is currently led by a dynamic principal and administrative team who have deep passion and commitment to the students and community. The teachers are bright-eyed and ready to get the year started. The school building (inside and out) looks ready to receive the bright young people who will enter its doors the following day. The last presentation given to the staff before they are given one final opportunity to prepare their classrooms is a discussion of equity issues and the moral imperative that they must confront as they seek to ensure that each student graduates high school prepared for college or work. About fifteen minutes into the discussion, a teacher says to the presenter, "Um, excuse me. but why are we talking about equity? I thought we had gotten past all of this stuff." You may be surprised that some staff members are unaware of the data context that should be shaping their understanding of the task that lies before them in educating students, but this is an all-too-common situation. The examination of this situation leads us to Key Action 3, acting on data to make instructional program decisions, and the principled practices that support it. It is impossible to pursue equity absent a context. Context in teaching and learning can be established most clearly by thoroughly understanding school and district data—quantitative and qualitative measures. The equity context is layered because there is a district context, a school context, and a classroom context, all of which need to be understood fully, not just by district leadership but throughout the organization. Furthermore, the data should have implications that are accessible to all who are responsible for influencing them—directly and indirectly. For instructional leaders, describing, unpacking, and connecting the district and school equity contexts is critical, but it is equally important that instructional leaders provide opportunities for their staffs to do the same.

The momentum that moves the school forward results from larger contexts (school or system patterns) becoming comingled with classroom-level trends. More specifically, if a school has data that show underrepresentation of boys in AP classes, the momentum to change that pattern happens when teachers see their own classroom cultures as connected to the school-level pattern. One of the most challenging barriers in pursuing educational equity is simply the ability to *see* the problems. Let's pause to make a critical distinction. The outcomes of a lack of equity may be readily visible, but the gaps in access that are contributing to those outcomes are typically not as visible, and those gaps are the problems that need to be addressed. For example, we may know that, as a school pattern, boys are more likely to be suspended than girls. What may be less visible to us is that materials being used in classes are of more interest to girls than boys. Furthermore, we may not be aware that in place of boys' academic engagement, they substitute social engagement. Citing disruptive behavior, teachers then refer boys to the office. Key Action 3 is about making the less visible areas (the access gaps) plainly visible as a standard school process. The frequent, regular use of data, both quantitative and qualitative, makes the schools' challenges more visible. Equity-focused instructional leaders need to make data-driven decisions the instructional norm.

Use Data in Daily Practice

Shifting the paradigm toward equity and access means that traditional practices will often have different purposes than in the past.

When using data on a daily basis, you will need to address directly how classroom observation data will be used. With the goal of access to quality instruction for each learner, leaders must convey that classroom observations are a means of collecting data that describe the *schoolwide* program. Shifting the culture so that the individual teacher receives benefit from classroom observations is pivotal to building instructional capacity. When implementing the PACE Framework, the classroom observation process needs to transform from traditional visits to "catch" teachers or to see "dog and pony shows" into forums for data collection and collaboration. The way that leaders conduct observations will have a significant impact on whether or not this change in practice occurs. Ideally, teachers and the administrative team will engage in observations as colleagues examining practice. These experiences will happen regularly and always have a discussion component that demonstrates the leader's commitment to analyzing instructional practice as a means of fostering teachers' professional growth and ability to meet the learning needs of each student.

As leaders deliberately work to change the environment, ensuring that feedback or discussions from observations are as valuable as feedback offered in a formal evaluation, they will accelerate the change in culture toward equity. Through consistent application, the cultural norms will shift to support shared responsibility for reflective practice. A climate cultivated with the expectation that teachers behave as instructional leaders in the classroom and the school community is paramount to equity transformation. A requirement for teacher leadership is active engagement and analysis of one's own practice. Teachers should be collecting data from every lesson that will illuminate the teaching and learning dynamic in their classrooms; this can be in the form of mental notes, written notes, and documentation of student participation, as well as traditional data, such as student performance on classwork, exit tickets, and the like. Leaders should make clear that an exchange should occur when they are conferring with teachers. A simple form can be used to keep the reflective discourse on track (see Figure 5.5).

Finally, the accountability that instructional leaders demonstrate in honoring this process change will speak volumes to staff. Because modeling is such an important means of showing value, consider how you, as the instructional leader, have engaged in reflective activity in between meetings with staff. How well versed will you demonstrate yourself to be as you offer other instructional options based on classroom visits? How will you demonstrate that you are applying an equity lens as you think about instructional practice? What are you willing to model or demonstrate so that staff members might see you as a resource in their journey?

Figure 5.5	Sample Teacher-Guided Reflection Template		

Date			
Grade/Course			
Description of How the Lesson Addresses the Instructional Vision			

Teaching Practices: Describe what you were doing. How did the school's equity imperative drive your practice?	Evidence of Student Learning: Describe how you assessed students' learning. Did you notice any students not making connections with what was taught or experienced?*	Next Steps: Based on evidence of students' learning, what will you do next (and why)?

What professional development (if any) do you think you need based on this discussion?

Follow-up discussion date (as needed):

*Requires discussion.

Instructional leaders move the trust needle when they help staff understand how they will be accountable in progress monitoring toward the preferred state of the teaching and learning dynamic. Because the movement we advocate is toward instructional partnership, part of this work involves taking the guesswork out of what it means for teachers to be held accountable in terms of demonstrated student growth on quantitative and qualitative indicators. Access to quality instruction for each student must be a norm, and leaders should support teachers and students toward this end. The purpose of classroom visits and observations is substantively different in a school or district that is leading for equity than in a school observing a traditional model. If the school community is to understand optimal conditions for engagement and instruction, then instructional leaders must call for copious examination of the school program. It is important to keep this goal in front of the team. Again, this is not a small consideration. It is an example of the kind of practice that will sustain the type of change you need in order to reach different outcomes. Furthermore, it is a significantly different mode of operation than we presently use in public education. Understanding the power of the teaching and learning dynamic through data is essential for determining the most effective evidence-based practices.

Expanding Sources of Data Over Time

As the practice on your campus or organization evolves, the use of data should become just a natural part of what happens in the building. Additionally, staff ideas about what qualifies as data should expand as well. This is how Key Action 3 supports the first two key actions, related to student engagement and relevance. When the instructional leader visits a class and notes that five heads are down on desks, that note becomes useable data. In traditional practice, leaders might not even notice students with their heads down on desks or what the impact could be on equitable learning outcomes. Often, the prevailing belief when this type of behavior is observed is that "Those are the kids who don't care" or "Those kids will be getting pulled out for resource soon." When as leaders we expand the definition of *data* to include assessments of engagement and we observe behaviors like heads down on a desk, there is a new discourse. The questions begin to shift. Leaders begin to ask questions like "Who were the five students with heads on their desks?" If they determine, for example, that four of the five are girls and three of the four are English language learners, then as instructional leaders for equity, we are positioned to look at the curriculum, the instructional practice, and the student learning activity through the lens of female English language learners. Then they can ask the question: "Was what I did today sufficient to meet their learning needs?" Furthermore, they can engage reflective partners and other instructional leaders, the first of whom should be instructional leaders leading for equity. Teachers and principals can have pointed conversations with their students to determine what their experience was. Teachers can then use the feedback from these discussions to adjust the learning environment the next day. They will not need to wait for an assessment that comes once every six weeks or once a year. Issues of access to a quality experience can be assessed on a daily basis. When these types of deliberations happen every day, as prompted by leadership pursuing educational equity, the organization's culture and effectiveness will transform in ways that support its current students, not those who went there a decade ago.

CONCLUSION

The imperative of ensuring access to quality instruction is an instructional leadership challenge for those pursuing educational equity. The limitation in opportunities for students to learn results from a range of factors, but one of the most critical is the failure of the educational community to prioritize student learning above all things. Schools exist to provide opportunities for young people to learn, grow, and develop. The pressures of change, the challenge faced when teachers are not adequately prepared to receive students from a wide range of backgrounds, and changing or shrinking resources are all modern-day realities faced in schools. The preparation requirements for active participation in our global system have only increased. Steadfast instructional leadership committed to quality in the classroom should focus on three areas: student engagement, instructional relevance, and robust accountability for student learning to meet today's challenges.

There is much discussion of the fact that teacher preparation must be reconceived in order to respond to changes in our student demographic. We agree that this is true; however, while that change is being discussed, groups of young people are showing up every day at our schoolhouse doors ready to learn. We don't need to wait for variables outside of our control to change before we prioritize the conditions most critical for students to learn. This chapter focused on what to prioritize and what discussions should sound like as a result of deliberate engagement around these critical factors with a focus on equity. Children who are behind don't have time to waste. Instructional leaders dealing with the urgency of now don't have time to wait. We believe that instructional leadership that is focused on students and access to quality instruction is what is needed to eliminate disparity in outcomes. Using the PACE Framework to prioritize student engagement and access to rigorous, relevant learning experiences offers a means for instructional leaders to get started on the work that will make a difference for children.

Principled Practices Summary

1. Instructional leaders pursuing educational equity must insist on actions that respond directly to conditions that create, maintain, or perpetuate achievement gaps. The necessity of student engagement, purposeful learning, and data-driven decision making are at the heart of efforts to close gaps in access.

2. The foundational beliefs of staff are critical; overlooking disparities in espoused versus demonstrated beliefs will undermine progress toward transformed practice. Instructional leaders must address dissonance in espoused beliefs and behaviors whenever they encounter it.

3. Moving equity into the classroom means creating a normative culture that unapologetically places student learning in the center. Instructional leaders must be clear on this point.

4. Instructional leaders must collaborate to collect and analyze data as a means of understanding the gaps in access that inform how practice needs to transform.

DISCUSSION QUESTIONS AND ACTIVITIES

1. The chapter opened with a discussion of student disengagement. Do the students in your school feel this way? How do you know how students feel about the level of engagement and/or relevance in instruction?

2. How do you assess what staff members in your building believe about children? What process do you use to challenge beliefs that are incompatible with the pursuit of high academic outcomes for each and every learner? What do you do when you encounter those who don't believe in the potential of each student?

3. As you think about engagement through the lens of cultural competence, what support has been provided to your staff so that cultural competence becomes the norm for them?

4. How is your team making cultural competence operative in your school? How are you describing the changes in teacher capacity? How are you addressing the development of your own personal level of cultural competence?

5. Take your leadership team on a learning walk of the school. Look for evidence (student work samples and products) that answer the question: "Why was the learning important?" After the learning walk, discuss what the team observed.

Types of Work Samples	Grade/Content Area	Demographic Breakdown of Student Samples Seen (e.g., race, gender, socioeconomic status, linguistic diversity, students receiving special education services)

6. What is your baseline assessment (*without reviewing any data— qualitative or quantitative*) of the percentage of your staff who effectively meet the teaching and learning needs of your students? Now compare that percentage with an actual percentage based on relevant data that describe student outcome measures. Were your perceptions accurate? Yes or no? If no, what did you observe about these teachers that led to your baseline assessment of their effectiveness?

7. If your assessment was accurate, what are the behaviors of these teachers that enable them to meet the needs of the student population effectively? Are these behaviors developed from university preparation, professional development, or in-school training, or are they behaviors that the teachers have figured out from trial and error? How do you create conditions to spread these behaviors among all staff?

Part III
Implementation and Beyond

6 The PACE Framework in Action

I am always ready to learn although I do not always like being taught.

—Winston Churchill

It was mid-June 2013, and principal Janice Proctor was getting teary eyed in her office as she reviewed the embargoed state assessment data. She was so disappointed that her student performance data had dropped in reading, mathematics, and science for all student groups. Proctor had thought she was being an effective leader by creating common planning for grade-level teams *and* vertical content teams. In her estimation, teachers had been invested in planning daily engaging lessons. As she opened up her desk drawer to locate a tissue, she wondered how to deliver the news about the data to staff. She also pondered how to continue to encourage her staff in light of the low scores. Given that the Common Core State Standards would also be implemented statewide the upcoming year, Proctor speculated that all this change could overload her school community.

Proctor's experience is similar to that of many principals in school districts across the nation. Like Proctor, most principals believe they are moving their school communities in the right direction. However, assessment data often indicate that student achievement is not progressing as intended. The PACE Framework assists principals in improving teaching and learning and, ultimately, student achievement. How ready are principals for the work involved in implementing the framework? This critical question is often overlooked because many principals are "doers." Typically, principals believe it is their duty to "get the work done." However, getting the work done does not always equate with getting the work done *well*. Specifically, how often do principals evaluate their efforts in terms of specific student outcomes? How often do principals pause and strategically determine the why, what, and how of the work ahead?

Accordingly, it is vital that you, as principal, step back and truly assess your readiness and your staff's readiness *before* taking any action (see Figure 6.1). Then, you can determine the appropriate pathway for implementing the PACE Framework in your school community.

GETTING STARTED: DETERMINING YOUR ENTRY POINT

The conditions within your school community should determine the appropriate implementation pathway into PACE. The entry points for implementation are associated with a four-phase continuum from pre-implementation to "deep implementation" (a phrase coined by Reeves, 2010):

Pre-implementation → Emerging Implementation → Developing Implementation → Deep Implementation

You can use insights gleaned from the readiness questions in Figure 6.1 to determine where your school is along this continuum. Figure 6.2 outlines some of the school conditions and requisite leadership next steps that may further help you to determine the appropriate implementation pathway and entry point for PACE.

Figure 6.1   How Ready Is Your School to Implement PACE?

1. Do stakeholders (teachers, students, and parents/guardians) have an understanding (using quantitative and qualitative measures) of the teaching and learning in your school? For example, who are the teachers? Who are the students? What is taught? How do students' narratives affect how they are taught?
2. Do stakeholders understand that school transformation is a process, not an event, and that the process takes time to create the necessary cultural norms?
3. Does the leadership team include at least one person knowledgeable about the processes needed to promote change?
4. Does the leadership team provide robust professional development plans?
5. In line with the Data-Driven, Student-Centered Framework for Achieving Educational Equity advanced in this book (see Figure 1.3), do performance data indicate that students are meeting and/or exceeding local, state, and national standards?
6. Do staff members value the use of data for instructional decision making?
7. Do staff members believe that each student in the building is capable of experiencing academic and behavioral success?

Figure 6.2   PACE Implementation Pathway

Implementation Pathway	Description
Pathway 1: Pre-implementation	*School Conditions* 1. Staff members do not regularly use disaggregated student achievement data to inform their instructional programs. The standard is always based on students meeting the expected outcome. 2. Staff members do not demonstrate a belief that each student can be academically and behaviorally successful (based on their words, actions, and/or student achievement data). 3. Staff members do not routinely meet to review disaggregated student achievement data in a structured fashion. 4. Staff members do not respond to disaggregated student data by engaging in meaningful, job-embedded, culturally responsive professional development. *Requisite Leadership Next Steps* 1. Develop a communication plan to build the case for school transformation. 2. Plan critical professional development relative to data collection and analysis, quality teaching and learning, collaborative teaming, and the relationship between student engagement and student learning. 3. Identify staff (varied by grade and content) that can help partner with the leadership team to move the work forward. 4. Create benchmarks to monitor implementation.
Pathway 2: Emerging Implementation	*School Conditions* 1. Staff members meet regularly to review disaggregated student achievement data with outcomes delineated; however, the outcomes are based on the expectation that some student groups will score lower because their starting point was much lower. Furthermore, meaningful instructional adjustments are not occurring. The data meetings require facilitation by administrators or resource staff. 2. Staff members believe that each student can be successful (based on their words, actions, and/or disaggregated student achievement data). 3. Staff members engage in multiple, job-embedded professional development activities; however, there is no focus on or accountability for changing behavior based on the professional development. *Requisite Leadership Next Steps* 1. Develop a communication plan to inform staff why the work must be refined. (Use the data to guide the conversation.) 2. Focus strategically on three to five equity-focused schoolwide learning objectives, and use these objectives to inform all professional development activities. However, the professional development plan must be responsive to needs realized as a result of the data collaborative planning sessions.

(Continued)

Figure 6.2 *(Continued)*

Implementation Pathway	Description
	3. Identify staff (varied by grade and content) that can help partner with the leadership team to move the work forward. 4. Create benchmarks to monitor implementation.
Pathway 3: Developing Implementation	*School Conditions* 1. Staff members meet regularly to review disaggregated student achievement data; however, the outcomes are based on the expectation that some student groups will score lower because their starting point was much lower. Additionally, meaningful instructional adjustments are not occurring. Generally, data meetings require structure and are run by teaching staff. There is little facilitation by administrators or resource staff. 2. Staff members believe that each student can be successful (based on their words, actions, and/or disaggregated student achievement data). 3. Staff (varies by grade and content) are identified to partner with the leadership team to move the work forward. 4. Staff members engage in multiple, job-embedded professional development activities. There appears to be a focus on and accountability for changing behavior based on the professional development; however, teacher practices are not changing. *Requisite Leadership Next Steps* 1. Organize a strategic planning committee to analyze progress and engage in a gap analysis of what is still needed to move the school forward. Review all elements to ascertain true gaps. If possible, consult with requisite district staff during planning meetings. 2. The strategic team must revisit the three to five equity-focused schoolwide learning objectives and the strategies associated with each. 3. Identify staff (varied by grade and content) that can help partner with the leadership team to move the work forward. 4. Revisit benchmarks set for implementation monitoring.
Pathway 4: Deep Implementation	*School Conditions* 1. Staff members meet regularly to review disaggregated student achievement data; however, the outcomes are based on the expectation that some student groups will score lower because their starting point was much lower. In addition, meaningful instructional adjustments are not occurring. The data meetings are run and organized by the teachers. A peer-appointed teacher records notes and next steps for the administrative team after each meeting. 2. Staff members believe that each student can be successful (based on their words, actions, and/or disaggregated student achievement data).

Figure 6.2 *(Continued)*

Implementation Pathway	Description
	3. Staff members engage in multiple, job-embedded professional development activities. There is a focus on and accountability for changing behavior based on the professional development.
	Requisite Leadership Next Steps
	1. Processes and structures are in place to guide the strategic planning committee. Membership is set, and there is a succession plan for staff who are in line for in-school and out-of-school promotions.
	2. Three to five equity-focused schoolwide learning objectives and the strategies associated with each have been set for the school community, and all work in the building is centered on meeting these objectives.
	3. Benchmarks are set for implementation monitoring. Various progress monitoring efforts are in place to facilitate the work.

Because determining the entry point into PACE implementation is a complex process, we examine April Smith's experiences in two different settings to highlight how principals *might* negotiate their entry into implementation. In 2006, Smith was promoted to a high-achieving, culturally diverse school community. The school community consisted of mid-career teachers. All teachers continuously received satisfactory evaluations; however, their lessons were traditional "stand and deliver" lessons. The teachers often suggested that there was no need to change their teaching because the students performed well on local, state, and federal assessments. The teachers maintained this stance even though significant gaps existed between student groups, especially the special education and African American student groups. Upon Smith's arrival, she realized quickly that there was no structured leadership team, school improvement team, or data meeting protocol. Furthermore, she learned that the teachers selected the professional development schedule for the following school year solely through an end-of-year survey.

Smith used the reflections and considerations in Figure 6.3 to identify the entry point for PACE as pre-implementation. Specifically, Principal Smith used the question-and-answer process outlined in Figure 6.4 to determine the appropriate PACE implementation pathway for her school community.

Smith's first principalship highlights a simple negotiation into PACE. However, the conversation becomes more textured when we review Smith's appointment to an underperforming school in 2009. Smith was selected as part of the state's turnaround agenda for persistently underachieving schools. The turnaround model is used when schools do not make their annual measurable objective for several years. The process allows a significant percentage of the staff, including the principal, to be evaluated. From this evaluation, it can be determined whether the staff are contributing to the students' underperformance. If so, then the staff are reassigned to another school community. If not, the staff are invited to stay at the school.

Figure 6.3	Determining the Entry Point for PACE Implementation: Reflections and Considerations

1. Are there any achievement gaps between and among students in your school?
2. Are there data indicating that teaching and learning is dynamic and responds to the needs of the students?
3. Do any systemic structures guide and inform the meetings occurring within your building?
4. Is there a fluid process that guides the professional development planning process? Are there opportunities to use various data sources during this process?
5. Do teachers believe they are doing a good job and that students are performing as they should (meaning there are no gaps among potential, skills, and actual performance)?

Figure 6.4	Negotiating Entry Into PACE Implementation (Principal Smith's First Principalship)

Question	Answer	Negotiation
Are there any achievement gaps between and among students in your school?	Yes	Given a yes response, all phases are potentially applicable.
Are there data indicating that teaching and learning is dynamic and responds to the needs of the students?	No	Given a no response, all phases except for deep implementation are applicable.
Do any systemic structures guide and inform the meetings occurring within your building?	No	Given a no response, pre-implementation and emerging phases are applicable.
Is there a fluid process that guides the professional development planning process? Are there opportunities to use various data sources during this process?	No	Given a no response, pre-implementation and emerging phases are applicable.
Do teachers believe they are doing a good job and that students are performing as they should (meaning there are no gaps among potential, skills, and actual performance)?	Yes	Given a yes response, the pre-implementation phase is most applicable.

Typically, this process involves a review of multiple data sources, community engagement, and a protocol governing the interview of the prospective principal.

Before Smith's assignment, the school community had engaged in robust improvement planning that included a comprehensive needs assessment and root cause analysis. Therefore, there was already a keen understanding of the students', teachers', and administrators' strengths and areas needing improvement. There were already structured data meetings, scheduled professional development, and a process in place to facilitate both. As Smith conversed with staff, the prevailing question asked was "If all of these great structures are in place, why is the school still underperforming?" After conversing with staff and cross-referencing multiple data points, Smith realized that staff did not fully appreciate the impact of the teaching and learning dynamic. More important, staff did not realize how lessons from the teaching and learning dynamic should impact the professional development schedule. Although many structures were in place, the structures did not use real-time data. The good news was that staff members wanted to do more. Regrettably, staff members were unsure of what that "more" entailed. Figure 6.5 illustrates Smith's question-and-answer process and how her process could determine the appropriate entry point into PACE implementation.

Figure 6.5	Negotiating Entry Into PACE Implementation (Principal Smith's Second Principalship)	
Question	**Answer**	**Negotiation**
Are there any achievement gaps between and among students in your school?	Yes	Given a yes response, all phases are potentially applicable.
Are there data indicating that teaching and learning is dynamic and responds to the needs of the students?	Yes	Given a yes response, all phases, except for the pre-implementation phase, are potentially applicable.
Do any systemic structures guide and inform the meetings occurring within your building?	Yes	Given a yes response, all phases, except for the pre-implementation phase, are potentially applicable.
Is there a fluid process that guides the professional development planning process? Are there opportunities to use various data sources during this process?	No	Given a no response, pre-implementation and emerging implementation phases are potentially applicable.
Do teachers believe they are doing a good job and that students are performing as they should (meaning there are no gaps among potential, skills, and actual performance)?	No	Given a no response, the emerging implementation phase is most applicable.

Principled Practices 1

1. Principals must be adaptive leaders. Leading through the unknown is the cornerstone of this work. Furthermore, adaptive principals own all challenges and confidently introduce these challenges to the school community as opportunities to be reflective and enhance practice. While implementing PACE, principals should lead confidently in the face of challenges such as a lack of clear structure for a new administrator and teacher evaluation process, the "in-development" teaching and learning framework, or "to be delivered at a later time" textbooks.

2. Principals must challenge their assumptions about students, teachers, parents/guardians, and the school community as a whole.

3. Principals must be reflective and be okay with saying, for example, "I did not do that" or "I did not do that well." The entry point to this work must include a true reflection of what knowledge and skills principals, teachers, students, and parents/guardians need in order to accelerate achievement for each student in every student group.

The negotiation outlined in Figure 6.5 led to an entry point in the emerging implementation pathway. The process of assessing the school community, the stakeholders' strengths and weaknesses, and the structures in place to implement PACE is complex. Although the principal must facilitate this negotiation, critical stakeholders should be included, such as teacher leaders, student leaders, parent/guardian advocates, and members of the school's leadership team. To that end, the introduction of the PACE Framework into a school community must be realized through the change management process.

LEVERAGING THE CHANGE PROCESS DURING PACE IMPLEMENTATION

According to Kotter (1996), 70 percent of all major change efforts in organizations are typically unsuccessful. This is true because many organizations, including schools, are unable to adapt continuously to change. Hence, the natural reluctance to adapt to change must be honored when principals introduce PACE into school communities (Fullan, 2001). Accordingly, we recommend that principals use Kotter's eight-step process for leading change when introducing PACE into their school communities (see Figure 6.6).

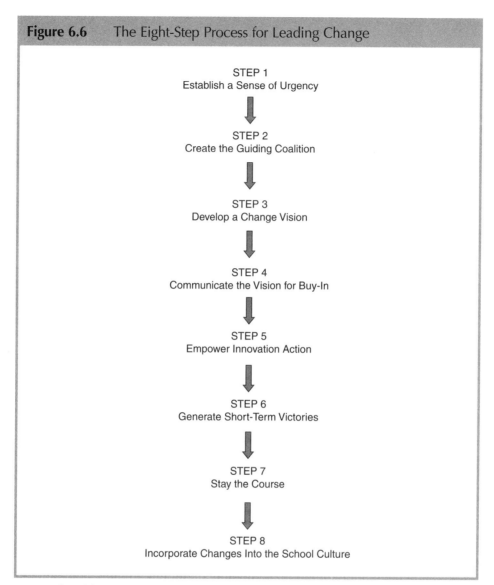

Figure 6.6   The Eight-Step Process for Leading Change

STEP 1
Establish a Sense of Urgency

STEP 2
Create the Guiding Coalition

STEP 3
Develop a Change Vision

STEP 4
Communicate the Vision for Buy-In

STEP 5
Empower Innovation Action

STEP 6
Generate Short-Term Victories

STEP 7
Stay the Course

STEP 8
Incorporate Changes Into the School Culture

Source: Adapted from Kotter (1996).

Regardless of the specific entry point into PACE, the change management process should be followed. If there is significant disagreement about why a framework like PACE is needed, heavy investment in steps 1 and 2 may be needed.

Each step requires a specific approach with very deliberate actions. In addition to assessing your school's readiness for PACE, you will need to assess your school community's positive attributes and use these attributes to leverage the change that is needed. Suggestions for how to do this work are integrated into the descriptions of each step that follows.

Step 1. Establish a Sense of Urgency

To engage in this vital work, it is absolutely essential that you establish a sense of urgency. Information gleaned from district-level priorities, new teacher and/or principal evaluation systems, student achievement data, perception data, discipline data, or a combination of any of these or other critical data can serve as the foundation for your sense of urgency. Given your staff's skill set, you must be extremely thoughtful about the approach used to create a sense of urgency. For example, Smith's first assignment required her to live in the nuances of the data. Specifically, the school community's aggregate student achievement data were impressive; however, the disaggregated data were less than stellar and revealed opportunities to enhance the school's instructional program.

Smith held a leadership retreat for all existing school-based leaders, as well as any teacher who was interested in reviewing the school's data. At the retreat, Smith distributed to all participants a data binder, which included a summary of student data, teacher assignments, student schedules, student disciplinary data, student participation in core programs, and the like. She divided the staff members into groups with a representative from each department and/or grade in every group. The groups were given a series of questions to guide the group discussion. The goal was to help them to see the gaps between and among student groups. The questions provided in Figure 6.7 are a sample of those that framed the group discussions. Groups were asked to record their responses and to be prepared to share their findings with the entire group.

Smith carefully observed and listened to discussions during the retreat. She took notes and asked clarifying questions. She also recorded the names of staff who (a) rallied others to agree with them, (b) articulated the nuances of the data, and (c) passionately communicated the voices of *each* student. The retreat was the *first* of several data analysis conversations. Smith used the names she recorded to designate informal leaders in the building, combined with district-level staff to facilitate the ongoing discussions.

Step 2. Create the Guiding Coalition

A school-based coalition must be created that can deliver the message to the invisible spaces within the school community (these include faculty rooms, teacher work rooms, hall duty, school social hours, and the like). This coalition must include respected members of the school community who may or may not always agree with the principal.

Figure 6.7   Data Discussion Questions: Peeling Back the Data

Understanding Student Achievement Data

1. Are there any achievement gaps between and among all students and each racial subgroup? If so, identify the gaps.
2. Are there any achievement gaps between and among students in the same subgroup? If so, identify the gaps.
3. Are there any achievement gaps between and among all students and the special education, free and reduced-price meal program, and limited English proficiency student groups? If so, identify the gaps.
4. Analyze student lists to determine which students are exposed to the core program and which students are exposed to interventions. Cross-reference these data with student performance data. What trends, if any, do you see?
5. Evaluate teacher assignments. What is the rationale driving teacher assignments to specific students or groups of students?
6. Evaluate student performance data by teacher. What do you learn? What structures do you have in place to address your analysis (i.e., who is teaching the students who are in need of the most instructional support)?
7. What trends are revealed in an analysis of student disciplinary data?

Understanding Adult Behavior That Influences Student Achievement

1. Do any systemic structures guide and inform the meetings that occur within your building?
2. Is there a fluid process that guides the professional development planning process? Are there opportunities to use various data sources during this process?
3. Do teachers believe they are doing a good job and that students are performing as they should (meaning there are no gaps among potential, skills, and actual performance)?

Such agreement is not central to this work. What is vital is agreement that the PACE Framework will be implemented in order to address student opportunity and/or achievement gaps. Quite frankly, challenging principals' perspectives and insights is often needed to keep the work fresh, progressive, and moving. Smith's identification of key staff during the leadership retreat served as the initial coalition to move this work forward.

Step 3. Develop a Change Vision

The school-based coalition, the principal, and district staff must create a detailed *change* vision. Specifically, the change vision must detail how structures will be revised, what strategies will be used to update the structures, and what monitoring processes will be used to assess the implementation and effectiveness of updated structures. Smith created a checklist of activities to engage in weekly, biweekly, and monthly. Her approach may appear technical and lack a response to the needs in the school, but it truly helped to keep her focused on the work. Principals must acknowledge

Principled Practices 2

1. Principals must include in their guiding coalitions individuals who challenge their way of thinking. These individuals may not be the most politically correct; however, true leaders can help them to grow.

2. Principals should include in their guiding coalitions a diverse group of stakeholders (with varying years of experience in and outside the school community, from various content areas, and with distinctly unique perspectives regarding how to move the work forward).

3. Principals must commit to creating a "safe space" for stakeholders to challenge existing norms, practices, and protocols with the ultimate goal of enhancing teacher practices and student performance.

their leadership gaps and then institute efforts to compensate for those gaps. Some principals may consider delegating this work, but we strongly discourage any delegation of change vision. To facilitate this work, Smith researched other similarly situated schools to examine their ability to eliminate gaps between and among student groups. She shared her findings with the guiding coalition. The coalition used lessons learned from other schools to frame the work for their change vision. The change vision became a standing agenda item at every coalition meeting. Figure 6.8 outlines the change vision used by Smith during her second principalship.

Step 4. Communicate the Vision for Buy-In

With the coalition as the guiding entity within the schoolhouse, a broad marketing plan must be created to communicate the change vision and modeling of new behaviors. A full investment in a marketing strategy is needed to inundate the school community with posters, logos, brochures, activities, and a widespread integration of the vision into existing practices and norms within the school community.

Figure 6.8   Sample Change Vision

Our school community will immediately challenge any rule, procedure, system, process, or structure that serves to undermine student achievement, disproportionally target one or more groups of students, or further the status quo behavior that created an ineffective culture of teaching and learning. We will proudly and boldly bring issues to the guiding coalition team to review and take immediate corrective action. Our work will be transparent and rooted in what is best for students and not in what is most comfortable for adults.

Smith used a grant to hire someone to provide an objective view of the work. This individual was charged with reviewing all programs, written materials, displays in the office and hallways, and any other available artifacts. Consequently, the school's internal and external communications were totally revamped. Note that there are several alternatives to hiring someone from outside the school community to conduct this type of review. Principals should consider district resources, community or university partners, and/or nonprofit organizations.

To uncover any disconnects between desired and actual practices, Smith ensured that all school procedures and practices were examined as well. For example, there was a common practice of using the school's intercom system to call into classes for early dismissals, conferences with school staff, and messages about picking up items from the office. As a result, the school instituted a procedure that the intercom system would be used only for emergencies during the last five minutes of class. Absent a school lock-down, all school announcements occurred only at the very beginning or end of the day. The examination of procedures and practices revealed several other disconnects between the vision and lived experiences within the school community. Smith was committed to ensuring that systemic practices were not allowed to undermine the work within the school community.

Step 5. Empower Innovative Action

Innovation may be perceived as a bad word within many public school communities. For instance, Smith could hear a pin drop when she asked teachers to share their ideas about how to do the work differently, how to engage students more fully, and how to rethink the infrastructure of the teaching and learning dynamic. Because of the belief that the status quo will continue, many teachers are conditioned to think that requests for innovation and "outside-the-box" thinking are unrealistic calls for input that will not transfer into any true action. If principals are serious about creating conditions for each student to be successful, as measured by multiple data points, the school community must be given the space to explore how to do this fluid and adaptive work. If not, more of the same will emerge and the achievement gap will persist.

Similar to the plan to communicate buy-in, a comprehensive campaign is needed to counter the idea that innovation is not wanted. A process to collect immediate feedback is warranted. Accordingly, Smith instituted an *optional* monthly survey to gain insight into existing processes and recommendations for improvement. Every meeting began and ended with a solicitation to give feedback to assist the school in achieving its vision more effectively. All feedback was recorded in the notes, and teachers were publically acknowledged for providing innovative ideas. Smith created a "You Took a Risk for the Benefit of a Child" award. Even when teachers' innovative ideas did not translate into a meaningful next step for the school community, Smith honored teachers for taking a risk. This culture shift is vital to encouraging innovative action by all.

Step 6. Generate Short-Term Victories

There must be a plan to demonstrate visible improvements from the inception of the PACE Framework. Stakeholders must be able to "see" the improvements. This means that achievable benchmarks of success must be conceived at the outset of PACE implementation to ensure that small wins are realized early in the transformation effort. Similar to Fullan's six secrets to change (Fullan, 2008), Smith created a culture to love her employees. To recognize and honor employees for their contributions to the work, Smith introduced the "You Are an Asset" protocol. She publically shared the reward system combined with short-term wins. Akin to student data walls that may be used when implementing PACE, a parallel structure is needed to showcase the short-term wins, including a list of all employees contributing to the wins.

This small but significant initiative created excitement around the work and slowly but surely transformed nonbelievers into believers. The power of creating small wins goes far in the world of "making change manageable" for those who typically shy away from change (and almost all individuals shy away from change). The short-term wins must be achievable, but they also must truly reflect a change in the work process. The wins must be credible. Therefore, principals must be intentional when creating short-term honors. Staff perception during this work matters!

Steps 7 and 8. Stay the Course and Incorporate Changes Into the School Culture

From the onset of implementing PACE, principals must strategically plan for the marketing of PACE, the sustainability of PACE, and the institutionalization of PACE into the core of the school culture. As Fullan (2001) suggests, organizations do not change; instead the people within the organizations change. Our work complements Fullan's research in that we assert repeatedly throughout this work that current teachers in public schools (the vast majority, at least) are the cavalry we are waiting on to transform schools. From the vantage point of PACE in action, principals serve as influential facilitators of PACE and, oftentimes, as thoughtful engineers of the work.

Smith enhanced her marketing plan to include rewards for teachers who attended school thirty days in a row and planned and implemented responsive lessons daily. Also, students were asked randomly in the hallway and during lunch breaks about their lessons. Moreover, teachers were asked to submit samples of student work daily and data from formative and summative assessments. (The teachers were given the names of students requiring work samples and formative and summative assessment data.) The information collected was cross-referenced to identify teachers who stayed the course. Furthermore, Smith reviewed the monthly perception surveys, team meeting minutes, department meeting notes, informal and formal observation data, and student achievement data to determine changes to the school culture. When changes were noted, the changes were incorporated into the weekly faculty bulletin and the monthly newsletter, displayed on the electronic display board in the hallway, and sent to the school community via automated success calls. However, such work alone is not sufficient. These efforts must eventually lead to equitable outcomes that contribute to eliminating the achievement gap.

The central component of this work is the willingness of principals, like Smith, to assume a multifaceted role. Principals must embrace an equity perspective in all they do. Furthermore, principals must function as instructional leaders, cheerleaders, strategic marketing consultants, and staff developers (to name just a few roles). Principals must have the requisite skill sets to negotiate the technical aspects of the work, as well as the organizational skills needed to keep the work moving. However, the most significant feature of PACE in action is principals' role as staff developer. In this instance, "staff developer" refers to the principal's ability to develop the staff assigned to his or her school. The ability to help staff see the urgency of the work, to build a coalition for moving the work forward, to progress monitor the work, to celebrate the successes along the way, and to institute successes into the fabric of the school culture is pivotal to realizing PACE in action.

CONCLUSION

This chapter opened with a description of Janice Proctor's experience, and we want to draw you back to her experience. Remember from the beginning that "Proctor thought she was being an effective leader by creating common planning for grade-level teams *and* vertical content teams. In her estimation, teachers were invested in planning daily engaging lessons."

PACE in action is an attempt to acknowledge the efforts of principals like Proctor while giving them a plan to engage critically in equity work. PACE provides a framework for approaching the idea of transformation using the infrastructure already established within any public school community. Although the implementation of PACE is complex, the structure provided in this chapter frames the work in a meaningful way for principals. The change management process needed to guide this work is fundamental to the successful implementation of PACE. It may be useful to consult additional references to build a comprehensive understanding of change management (see previously cited works by Fullan and Kotter). However, it is unproductive for principals to continue to suggest that exterior barriers, such as district policies and procedures, limited resources, and potentially a compromised professional development program, are the cardinal reasons for their inability to do what is right by children. For principals who are committed to teaching each student well, PACE is a distinct opportunity that takes into account students' demographic characteristics, learning needs, and/or readiness for learning.

Principled Practices Summary

1. Instructional leaders must assume the role of change agent. They must own the change process. Specifically, they must eliminate fears by openly acknowledging the staff's skills to manage the impending change.

2. Instructional leaders should assess the strengths of their staff and then determine the appropriate entry point for implementing the PACE Framework.

3. Instructional leaders should clearly identify their guiding coalition—that is, their partners—in moving this work forward. They should also operationally define the work by creating a clear plan with benchmarks, metrics of success (delineating expected short-term wins), and expected end-of-year outcomes.

4. Instructional leaders must organize themselves for instruction by adhering to the implementation plan they create. They must be relentless in working toward the outcomes outlined in the plan.

DISCUSSION QUESTIONS AND ACTIVITIES

1. Ponder what you know about your school community. Identify what practices and structures are in place to potentially guide the PACE Framework in action.

2. Is there any organizational change precedent that might govern or assist in guiding the implementation of the PACE Framework in your school community?

3. What external resources are available to assist you in implementing the PACE Framework (for example, knowledgeable district-level staff, student data systems, teacher evaluation systems, additional resources)?

4. Is a small group of district-level professionals available to coach you through this process? If yes, invite them to all conversations regarding implementation of the PACE Framework to ensure that they have an authentic context for the work.

7

Institutionalizing the PACE Framework to Realize a Transformed Schooling Process

So if we are to remain globally competitive in today's world, we need to produce more than just a few entrepreneurs and innovators. We need to develop the creative and enterprising capacities of all our students.

(Wagner, 2012)

About three years ago, Jeanne Brown contacted her school district's central office in dismay. She was a new principal at a middle school in the suburban part of a rapidly urbanizing school district. Brown shared that her school community had changed significantly both racially and socioeconomically over recent years, but the previous administration appeared to have done nothing in response to the changes. The school had zero-tolerance suspension policies; it used inflexible, homogeneous ability grouping based largely on teacher recommendation; and students of color and those from poverty were significantly underrepresented in advanced courses. Despite all the school community changes, from what Brown could tell, there had been no professional development, no practice or policy change, and no evaluation of how the changing population should affect daily practice. In an exasperated voice, she told the district officer, "If we continue to operate like this, there is no way our school will remain competitive."

According to Govindarajan and Trimble (2010), "All competitive advantages inevitably decay. Companies that resist change, those that fail to innovate soon die. Therefore, strategy cannot be about maintaining the status quo. It must be about creating the future. In other words, strategy is innovation" (p. 8). This is the moment in which we in public education find ourselves. Many schools and districts that used to serve majority white, majority middle-class families are changing. School districts across the county are becoming more racially, ethnically, socioeconomically, and linguistically diverse. Demographers predict that this trend will continue throughout the twenty-first century. In this book we have offered ideas, processes, and practices for responding to these changes. One thing is for sure, the status quo has proven itself ineffective practice for leaders seeking to eliminate achievement disparities.

Many are choosing to deny that changes in families, communities, and society in general should have any bearing on how we undertake the daily business of schooling. They say things like, "Why should we consider race? We live in a post-racial society," or "Why should we consider class? All things are equal when young people come to our school," or "Why should we think about the performance of our English language learners? Not everyone goes to college." This type of thinking, though practiced widely, should be judged against educational outcomes. The data tell us that we are not serving all student groups well. What the data don't tell us is what we need to do about it. This book was written to enable readers to take action in response to what the data are telling us, to defy common ways of thinking and responding to achievement challenges. To respond to inequities in educational outcomes we must take deliberate steps to ensure equity in both access and opportunity. The transformation that needs to happen in public education needs to happen now. We need to be the ones who respond to the urgent need for change.

The PACE Framework was created, in part, to engender academic conversation about what works using an equity lens. The extension of the "what works" conversation is the emphasis on evidence of effectiveness. In implementing the framework, instructional leaders should ensure, to the extent possible, that outcomes are attributable to either (a) the instruction provided or (b) the use of instructional time for active engagement of students. In order to develop this type of understanding of the school or district educational program, a systemic structure is essential. Use of these two data points allows leaders to advance conversations about learning as a condition of teaching and instructional practice. The focus is on evidence-based practice. Why is this so important? Think about the many conversations you have had in which something in teaching and learning goes either really well or really poorly and no one can describe what the original instruction intended. Can you recall debriefing a lesson during a post-observation conference and realizing that the teacher had not thought about possible student responses to the instructional prompts? Have you been involved in discussions with staff about lessons in which there was no deliberate plan to compel students to want to learn? The PACE Framework supports the coupling of teaching and learning and evidence-based practices, acting our way to equity.

WHY INSTITUTIONALIZE THE PACE FRAMEWORK?

By institutionalizing PACE, you ensure that the types of discussions described above occur less frequently over time and ultimately become nonexistent in your school or organization. The urgency of our achievement challenges means that we don't have time for activities that don't work. The use of instructional time should be linked to defensible, not historical, practices. Underserved students are telling us that our daily practices are ill suited to the achievement challenges of a rapidly changing public school population. The PACE Framework enables you to use an equity lens to create the conditions needed to systematically address the transformation process. The framework is designed to address daily access to quality instruction for each student as realized through assessment of real-time data.

This chapter describes three critical principles for taking the PACE Framework from implementation to institutionalization to deepen transformation efforts:

1. Making dominant practices visible

2. Applying the equity lens consistently

3. Building in accountability, inspecting forward progress

The guiding change theory in this book is based on the concept of "principal as instructional leader for equity." Principals who engage in daily instructional leadership are central to school transformation efforts because of the critical importance of access to quality instruction. These principals create school standards and give permission to staff to change to meet the needs of every student. At the school district level, school superintendents and CEOs function similarly. Hence, in order to change patterns of inequity permanently, leadership from the top of the organization must show the way.

As you move your campus or organization forward in pursuing educational equity, it is important to keep your eye on two priorities: (a) the ways in which the organization needs to change and (b) the structures needed to support that change (Kotter, 2011). These priorities can best be described as change leadership (the vision of the change) and change management (structures supporting change). As you move deeper into implementation of PACE, it is important to take stock of how you see the classroom environment, the students and the teachers, and the school community changing. How you affectively experience the school or district change coupled with empirical data will offer the leverage you need to make decisions about the most critical ways forward. According to Fullan (2011), "Thinking and feeling practitioners are the only ones who can find ways to break through inertia" (p. 3).

Implicit in the change leadership–change management evaluation are two questions for your school community: (a) What needs to change? and (b) What needs to stay the same? Engage your leadership coalition in brainstorming of these two ideas. Figure 7.1 offers a tool to frame the team's deliberations as you journey deeper into the critical aspects of change leadership–change management needed to move from implementation to institutionalization of PACE.

Notice in Figure 7.1 that the line between the up and down arrows is not at equilibrium. This is because as we consider change leadership–change management, we see that balancing practices that need to change and those that do not may result in a lack of equilibrium. The use of an equity lens to frame deliberations should define how we seek balance.

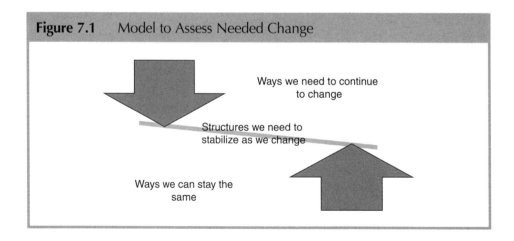

Figure 7.1   Model to Assess Needed Change

Ways we need to continue to change

Structures we need to stabilize as we change

Ways we can stay the same

As leaders, making the calculations necessary to enhance the likelihood of successful change is as important as advancing the needed change. For example, some practices, such as tracking students into low-level courses or applying harsher discipline to male students, may need to be extinguished immediately. The critical issue is to leverage sufficient stability to engender successful change. Leadership teams can use Figure 7.1 to engage in this analysis. The learning from implementation of PACE coupled with your team's observations should help the team to make the necessary decisions. We break with the framework that suggests change in a state of "all things being equal." Pursuing equity is not synonymous with equality. In making assessments of change needed to achieve equity, be prepared to directly have conversations about the need for differential treatment that responds to the needs of students. Figure 7.1 is meant to prompt your consideration of the critical nature of decision making as you journey toward institutionalized practice. The sections that follow unpack the key principles of change leadership and change management that are especially salient to institutionalizing transformed instructional practices while ensuring enhanced achievement outcomes.

CHANGE LEADERSHIP–CHANGE MANAGEMENT PRINCIPLE 1: MAKING DOMINANT PRACTICES VISIBLE

The clarity in vision of quality teaching and learning, of assessing the current state of teaching and learning, and of consistently engaging in capacity-building activities, all while ensuring accountability, are regular aspects of operations in schools implementing the PACE Framework. The question of how a school moves from implementation to institutionalization is essential for transformation. The key goal of the PACE Framework is to *eliminate the access gap* by purposefully ensuring every student has access to quality instruction and engaging learning opportunities. Eliminating achievement gaps is impossible without understanding and effectively addressing gaps in access (Carter & Weiner, 2013). The most critical gap in the schooling of underserved students is the perpetual series of unavailable/inaccessible opportunities to learn. Identifying these gaps in access to learning opportunities can be difficult because policies, practices, and procedures are generally crafted from a posture of neutrality. In other words, we seldom consider the impact that our policies, practices, and procedures have on equitable outcomes. We assume that these structures have equal impact on all students. The principle of making the dominant narrative visible is all about bringing into question policies (at the district level) and practices and procedures (at the school level) in order for institutional transformation to occur.

An example of this principle in practice can be illustrated through the experience of Vicki Stevens, a third-year principal at a relatively high-achieving high school. Stevens and her leadership team began preparing for the third year of her principalship much in the way she had in prior years—by reviewing data. One of the areas of concern that she and her team discussed was Advanced Placement (AP) participation trends. The shared vision for the school community was that participation in AP course offerings would, minimally, be proportionate to the demographic composition of the student population. Despite increasing course offerings over the years, participation data were relatively flat. Poor students and black and brown students were significantly underrepresented. The leadership team talked about the significant amount of reading that was required in the AP classes and how that served as a barrier for many students. Stevens asked about how teachers were working with the middle school to ensure that students were building their reading stamina before they got to high school. The ninth-grade team described how they were addressing this challenge in their articulation efforts with the middle school. They also shared how reading volume had been enhanced among the high school students as well. Stevens was perplexed. Their practices should have been helping students manage the rigor of the AP courses, but again the data were not showing any changes. The leadership team decided to have meetings with grade-level teams to discuss this trend. They asked each team to describe the process they were using to increase the volume of reading required of students. During these meetings, the administrators found some interesting trends. First, each grade-level team was managing the reading task in a very different way. Some were providing more reading at students' instructional levels; some were providing more at independent levels. Some were connecting writing assignments; others were not. Within the group that was connecting reading and writing, some were having students write formally, while others were having students complete only quick-writes. Practices were all over the spectrum with staff of the same school.

There had been no planning to ensure continuity or consistency among efforts from grade to grade. Second, data showed that students assigned the most reading were those deemed "highly able" or "gifted" by the middle school. This group of students represented a fairly small percentage of the overall student population (5 percent). Furthermore, according to the team's plans, these students were by no means a full representation of the scope of students who should end up in AP classes during their junior and senior years. Therefore, the larger goal of increasing students' reading volume was being addressed inconsistently. Furthermore, an invisible track of students had been created as the community pursued the larger goal. If this behavior had remained invisible, the school team's efforts to increase participation in AP courses surely would have remained futile. Pause here and think about how you can deepen implementation of PACE into your organization's infrastructure. Use the reflection in Figure 7.2 to make certain that a clear connection between practices and outcomes can be made.

Moving Into Institutionalized Practice: Making Common Practices Visible

In order to transform school and district practices strategically in ways that disrupt the demographically predictable underservice of diverse students, leaders need a protocol for unearthing the sources of the inequality. Figure 7.3 describes a four-step method for evaluating common practices. First, the challenge needs to be named. In the earlier example, Stevens found that AP courses did not have demographically proportionate participation. As you consider changing common practices, you must make certain that a clear connection between practices and outcomes can be made.

Step 2 includes identifying specific policies, practices, and procedures designed to address the challenge. Conducting a thorough audit of each part of the policy, practice, procedure, or program is step 3 of the process. At this step, gaps, disparities, and inconsistent interpretations may emerge.

Figure 7.2   Reflection

Identify a policy, practice, or procedure that you have audited using an equity lens. After the identification and analysis, name the insight that you otherwise would not have had.

Figure 7.3   Four-Step Method for Evaluating Common Practices

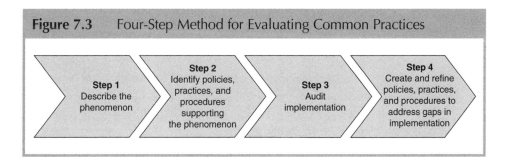

The result of this type of analysis is the kind of understanding needed to make the implementation of PACE rich and meaningful in a school community. It is part of the process that begins to remove the layers that "wallpaper" our understanding of how inequity is maintained and perpetuated in schools and districts (Johnson & LaSalle, 2010). In the example discussed earlier, Stevens and her team revised how they articulated with the middle school and standardized (at each grade level) the types of reading and writing assignments that would serve as enhancements. The team continued to systematically refine reading enhancements and assignments by grade and subject area over time. They were methodical and deliberate in ensuring that students had access to specific types of reading and writing experiences that were scaffolded to engender preparation for the rigors of AP courses. Teachers received training and support in using culturally relevant pedagogy to ensure increasing opportunities for relevant, engaging learning were available.

Now imagine Stevens's experience without closer investigation. The systemwide practice made sense given the barriers that teachers identified regarding students' challenges in AP courses. However, only through deeper consideration were cracks in daily access unearthed. As we move from implementation to institutionalization of PACE, we need to ensure that we act on what is happening, not on what we think is happening. Job-embedded professional development provided in this context improves teacher effectiveness because training is related directly to student outcomes. Over time, the school or system builds the type of infrastructure that supports continuous school improvement. Unlike traditional school improvement, in which inequities are hidden in the aggregate, this type of improvement process focuses on examination of gaps (what is believed versus what is observed and what can be quantified), which then creates the context essential to continue the work of eliminating achievement gaps.

Principled Practices 1

1. Exercise change leadership and change management at the same time. As you create more equitable practices and processes, it is critical for change to be managed.

2. Be clear on what requires visionary leadership (what needs to be created that does not exist) as well as on parts of the change process that need regular attention and management.

CHANGE LEADERSHIP–CHANGE MANAGEMENT PRINCIPLE 2: APPLYING THE EQUITY LENS CONSISTENTLY

One of the most widespread school and system beliefs is the assumption that equity is naturally embedded in the tools we use systemwide. We assume that equity and fairness are embedded in our curriculum development processes, our instructional practices, our discipline practices, and the like. Yet what is embedded in conducting daily public schooling is inequity. Inequity is embedded because schools were not created to serve the population of students who largely comprise today's student bodies. This creates the imperative to consistently apply an equity lens to our decision making. Using the Data-Driven, Student-Centered Framework for Achieving Educational Equity (see Figure 1.3) in order to understand unintended consequences that may be occurring as we seek to serve each student is a means of consistently applying that lens. Leaders institutionalizing educational equity practices need to use an equity lens regularly across the school or organization. Figure 7.4 lists four critical questions that leaders can ask themselves and their leadership teams as they assess movement from implementation to institutionalization of the PACE Framework.

Moving Into Institutionalized Practice: Probing Deeply to Inspect Evidence of Daily Use of an Equity Lens

As you start to see the achievement/outcomes gaps narrow in your school or district, you should feel confident and emboldened that you're well on your way to a transformed organization. However, be mindful that the goal of transformation is to eliminate the conditions that are causing or perpetuating disparities. The tables in Figure 7.4 are designed to show your class, school, or district's progress and opportunities. The next step toward institutionalization must involve taking stock. PACE is designed to keep leaders and their staffs focused on the work of daily quality instruction for each student. Taking stock of progress is critical to the transformation to equitable practice. Now the work is to dive in more deeply by asking probing questions.

Probing questions are those that take leaders and their staffs further into the development of cultural competence with the goal of creating a *student/community/conscious organization.* A student/community/conscious organization is one in which the school's staff has "right" cultural knowledge. "Right" cultural knowledge is exemplified by thinking that does not marginalize or subordinate perspectives that are different from that which has been normalized. It does not proffer stereotypes and prejudices.

Figure 7.4   Is the Equity Lens Becoming Institutionalized Practice in Our School?

1. Given our implementation efforts, I observed the following examples of the use of the equity lens in our efforts:

2. What are the data that corroborate our use of the equity lens?

Outcome Data	Evidence That Gaps Are Closing

Outcome Data	Evidence of Challenges That Remain

3. How are we communicating the degree to which we see the equity lens being used?

4. How will we move forward in those areas in which we've noted inconsistencies?

Principled Practices 2

1. Act on the knowledge that equity cannot be embedded into policies, practices, and procedures that are, in substance and form, marginalizing.

2. Until policies, practices, and procedures have been transformed, always apply an equity lens to assessments of effectiveness.

To the contrary, intellectually curious leaders and teachers transitioning toward equity examine questions like "To what degree is racial difference impacting achievement?" and "To what degree are class differences impacting achievement?" and "To what degree are linguistic differences impacting achievement?" Furthermore, when those questions are presented, the dispositions of those engaged in the conversation need to be open and inquiring rather than defensive and dismissive.

Developing a student/community consciousness in the context of the global challenges of the twenty-first century is a hallmark of the transformation process in public education. Many forces influence the way we engage in the schooling process. Movement toward institutionalization means, in part, creating a climate that is conducive to the change. Applying the equity lens daily will require deliberate development of cultural knowledge, skill, and disposition. Evidence of cultural knowledge can then become a factor in hiring decisions, evaluation decisions, and daily practice decisions. The mode of operations of the school will become so transparent that attracting "right-fit" candidates will be far easier than before the school or district undertook its equity work.

CHANGE LEADERSHIP–CHANGE MANAGEMENT PRINCIPLE 3: BUILDING IN ACCOUNTABILITY, INSPECTING FORWARD PROGRESS

We focus on access to quality instruction because we contend that the environment for teachers to become powerful accelerators of student achievement can be created through bold, sophisticated instructional leadership. That instructional leadership must prioritize equity and inspect the progress it expects. Once achievement outcomes change, beliefs about possibilities for each child will change. This is the potential outcome of all the work that you have invested in as you have moved through this book. The third change leadership–change management principle relates to accountability for forward progress.

Here's a situation that illustrates this principle in action. Principal Wright found herself conferring with her social studies department chairperson about data describing tenth-grade students' performance on research-based capstone projects, which demonstrated significant disparities in student outcomes. The social studies department was taking the lead in developing a model for engaging students in rigorous research through completion of capstone projects. Through implementation of the PACE Framework in the previous school year, the leadership team, with the consensus of teachers and with feedback from students, determined that research projects (capstones) would be the major area of focus and implementation to support the school mission. These research projects would be designed to provide ideas to community stakeholders on solutions to community problems. Feedback from the students on the initiative was that the capstone project was absolutely necessary since a part of the school's mission was to uplift the community in which the school was located. Everyone was excited about infusing these types of activities into the academic work for each student. Authentic, purposeful learning supported by the students and teachers was precisely the type of project that Wright had in mind. The fact that next steps in pursuing a quality instructional program were emanating from student feedback and was indicative of rigorous engagement was exactly what the team had worked so diligently for during the first year of implementation of the PACE Framework.

The social studies department hit a challenge about a third of the way into the project. Teachers and students were collaborating across disciplines. Students were using technology to connect with other students who were exploring ideas similar to theirs. If students chose a community challenge that was related to the environment (for example), they were paired with a science advisor. Wikis were used for student/teacher/community chats. Each research area had a wiki site devoted to its issue. Students began to group themselves according to their areas of interest as they socialized in the cafeteria. Periodically teachers were observed having lunch with students. Many lunch chats revolved around passionate discussions of the challenges students were investigating. Students were also engaging in individually directed reading on concepts related to their problems of interest. The students' research activities were broadening their scope of knowledge on their topics. For all intents and purposes, this initiative "looked like" the vision of real learning that all the stakeholders had agreed was most powerful.

The challenge arose when the teams (first the social studies department, then the leadership team) began analyzing student performance data. Among those completing capstone projects, 80 percent of Hispanic students were on track to receive a score of less than proficient a third of the way through the project as assessed by the rubrics mutually agreed on by students and teachers. The social studies department and the leadership team worked to analyze why an activity that was so engaging to students was not lending itself to similarly high performance outcomes. First, staff reviewed data that described teachers' adherence to practices that supported the school vision of quality instruction. The information examined included summations of observed teacher practices and data describing critical aspects of student engagement, such as choice and students' interest. These data didn't provide any real clues.

The social studies department team decided to analyze the topics selected by the Hispanic students. They wanted to determine if there was some barrier created by the topic selection; they used a racial lens to examine this question. Their analysis showed that a general theme characterized a disproportionate percentage of research projects for Hispanic students. Hispanic students were overwhelmingly interested in the growth of what they perceived as aggressive policing practices that were directed toward populations of color and immigrants (65 percent of students were examining some variation of this issue). Hispanic students' performance data were showing consistent patterns of not meeting the standard of "evidence that the area of study is a community problem" based on the rubric. These students characterized their studies as an examination of issues that were unique to a community that serves high percentages of immigrants of color. Students were consistently finding a lack of evidence that spoke to the presence of many community issues that were relevant from their perspective. Students examined data related to "stop and frisk" (a policing practice) of individuals from areas where high numbers of limited English speakers and people of color congregated. As the students completed their projects, they contended with the unique challenge of "lack of empirical evidence." In other words, for these students, many of the community issues relevant to them and their families were not those recognized by our larger community structures. Many students undertaking this research topic found that data that in other cases might be retrieved by way of a simple Freedom of Information Act request from a government agency was unavailable to them. After this trend was discovered, teachers and students worked to refine studies to enhance the students' abilities to examine their area of interest. As a result of this group's interest, the teachers added a unit on survey design in the next iteration of this task. Once this barrier was removed, Hispanic students' performance was on par with their peers.

This example illustrates two critical issues related to institutionalizing the PACE Framework. First, the outside environment (community, society, economy, and the like) and the skills needed to be successful are always changing. Technology is rapidly accelerating societal change. Embedding PACE in the scope of operations of a school or a system of schools will give principals a fluid mechanism to respond to these changes. Notice, in the example above, that the students didn't fail the course nor did they abandon their interest. Staff investigated ways to engender students' success in the presence of—not the absence of—their personhood, their culture. The use of education to affirm our diverse students' efforts is something our unchallenged historical systemic practices don't accomplish. Instructional leaders pursuing equity should professionally reflect on areas of difference that diversity factors offer to the teaching and learning tasks of their staff and students. Actively working to build depth of knowledge of students and communities is critical to enable leaders to make decisions about how schooling should be shaped in service to its stakeholders. When these areas of difference are uncovered, the leadership challenge in the subsequent phase of instructional program implementation is to build capacity of staff to engage in what Fullan (2011) calls, "impressive empathy," which he defines as "the ability to put yourself in other people's shoes, particularly those who hold values and experiences very different than yours" (p. 30).

Second and more implicit is the needed evolution of how education is conceptualized and realized in practice. The instructional leader for equity endeavoring to institutionalize PACE must work to reset the educational default position from a middle-class, Eurocentric focal point to the prism of cultural, social, and economic diversity. As PACE becomes the way a school or system operates, new policies, practices, and procedures should be conceived from evidence of the successful practices that rigorously engage each student in relevant learning. In this work, considering the needs of underserved students is not secondary; it happens as a central part of the organization's operations. Resetting the practice default is an undertaking that requires passion, grit, and process. Leading for equity requires that we keep an eye on this movement. It is not hyperbole to describe this work as everyday activity; it can, however, be done.

Moving Into Institutionalized Practice: How to Get Closer Every Day to Realizing the Possibilities for Each and Every Student

The accountability needed to transform our schools to meet the needs of each student will have to be self-selected and self-imposed in many cases. The case of the social studies department described earlier illustrates a significant nuance related to access that a traditional state or local accountability system would not be able to identify. The nuance was the understanding of how social culture intervenes in the teaching and learning process, how race and ethnicity can be powerfully used in teaching and learning. In many schools and districts, aggregate trend data are used widely to assess progress, but consider the problematic nature of using aggregate data to understand the community-specific perspective that students were using to complete the research assignment. Leaders looking only at aggregate data would never be positioned to make the types of adjustments critical to supporting each student's success on that activity.

Leaders working to institutionalize practices that are equitable will need to create progress monitoring and benchmarking systems that show disaggregated outcomes. Transforming practices toward equity using PACE requires the school community to grow in understanding how disparities in outcomes are shaped by disparities in inputs and opportunities. To get closer and closer to schoolwide equitable outcomes, the school community must enhance its collective ability to deal with the impacts of nuance. The complexity and complication inherent in understanding nuance is considerable. When we begin to consider racial, cultural, social, political, and geographical differences and how these shape experiences in teaching and learning, we can appreciate the nuances in teaching and learning.

Helping staff to understand what disparities in achievement outcomes mean in the lives of students is as much a part of the presentation of data as are discussions of what should be done about the disparities. Instructional leaders need to help staff intellectually, emotionally, and cognitively connect to what the data mean. After that shared understanding has been developed, leaders must then set next steps that are both measurable and observable. The idea is not to throw a litany of strategies and programs at the school's challenges. Instead, persistence combined with a broadened understanding of the range of available instructional responses equals a different, deepened course of action. All actions should be judged by outcomes. Regardless of the intention, the third principle is about the kind of accountability that honors inputs and quality thinking but is sober in its focus on the achievement of goals.

Principled Practices 3

1. Create accountability systems that supersede federal, state, and local requirements.
2. Ensure accountability systems have an infrastructure that allows the community to understand *access,* not just outcomes.

CONCLUSION

Several key principles are necessary to ensure that the gains you make in implementation of PACE are continued as you move toward institutionalization. Managing change while you lead, changing policies, practices, and procedures, and then creating accountability that represents ideals for your students are essential components of the journey to institutionalize the PACE Framework. The need to be aware of how your school or organization is functioning (at a variety of levels) as assessed by outcomes for students is essential. This knowledge positions your community to continually make purposeful decisions that provide each student with the opportunity for an appropriate and responsive educational experience. Knowing what is working for your students will also enable your staff to concentrate on the practices that make the difference. It will be easier to know which programs or practices can be discontinued or avoided because you will be clear about what is absolutely essential in fostering each student's learning. Finally, the most important aspect of moving into institutionalized practices that are aiding your development into an organization achieving equity and excellence is that these practices become the norm. Differences between and among our students don't have to be deficits, nor do they have to lead to deficiencies. The work to institutionalize equitable practice using the PACE Framework is all about demonstrating that student differences don't have to be educational dilemmas; indeed, they are opportunities.

Principled Practices Summary

1. Instructional leaders focused on equity must manage change and lead change simultaneously as they institutionalize PACE. Both are crucial to institutionalized transformation.

2. Education leaders must transform policies, practices, and procedures that lead to disparate achievement outcomes. To prevent regression to old, ineffective practices, evidence-based practice should become the organizational norm.

3. Leading for equity will require more than minimum compliance requirements. Floor-level accountability will only frustrate efforts to move the school community forward. Being unapologetically focused on standards that correlate to success after K–12 will help the organization permanently change its function.

DISCUSSION QUESTIONS AND ACTIVITIES

1. The first principled practice is about effective change leadership and change management. With your team, describe the formal structure you use to manage the change process in your school or district. Name a practice that was transformed significantly during implementation and then institutionalization of PACE. What made this effort successful? How can you replicate or expand on this success?

2. How has your consistent implementation of PACE led to refining your vision of quality teaching and learning? How have you worked to change or adjust procedures or practices associated with your school community's ability to achieve this vision? How are disparities in achievement outcomes being impacted? Is there evidence that changed practices and procedures are being implemented throughout the school or district? If yes, describe the evidence.

3. Are there programs or resources that warrant examination as a result of any changes in practices or procedures? Does the leadership team have a plan of action if it is determined that a program or resource should be discontinued because it is not supporting equitable achievement outcomes?

4. How does the accountability system used in your school go beyond local and state accountability? In quantitative and qualitative terms, describe the metrics you are using and how these exceed local and state accountability metrics.

5. Describe how the school (district) accountability systems allow your staff to assess access and gaps in learning opportunities. What equity goals will you pursue based on the progress your team has had thus far?

List of Figures

References

Introduction

Aud, S., Hussar, W., Johnson, F., Kena, G., Roth, E., Manning, E., ... Notter, L. (2012). *The condition of education 2012* (NCES 2012–045). Washington, DC: U.S. Department of Education, National Center for Education Statistics.

Aud, S., Hussar, W., Kena, G., Bianco, K., Frohlich, L., Kemp, J., & Tahan, K. (2011). *The condition of education 2011* (NCES 2011–033). Washington, DC: U.S. Department of Education, National Center for Education Statistics.

Boykin, W., & Noguera, P. (2011). *Creating the opportunity to learn: Moving from research to practice to close the achievement gap*. Alexandria, VA: ASCD.

Federal Interagency Forum on Child and Family Statistics. (2013). *America's children: Key national indicators of well-being, 2013*. Retrieved from http://www.childstats.gov/americaschildren/famsoc1.asp

Heifetz, R. A., Linsky, M., & Grashow, A. (2009). *The practice of adaptive leadership: Tools and tactics for changing your organization and the world*. Boston, MA: Cambridge University Associates.

Louis, K., Leithwood, K., Walstrom, K., Anderson, S., Michlin, M., Mascall, B., ... Moore, S. (2010). *Learning from leadership: Investigating the links to improved student learning*. Retrieved from http://www.wallacefoundation.org/knowledge-center/school-leadership/key-research/Pages/Investigating-the-Links-to-Improved-Student-Learning.aspx

Singleton, G., & Linton, C. (2006). *Courageous conversations about race: A field guide for achieving equity in schools*. Thousand Oaks, CA: Corwin.

Warne, R., Godwin, L., & Smith, K. (2013). Are there more gifted people than would be expected in a normal distribution? An investigation of the overabundance hypothesis. *Journal of Advanced Academics*, 24(4), 224–241.

Chapter 1

Aldridge, S. (2003). The facts about social mobility. *New Economy, 10*, 189–193.

Aud, S., Hussar, W., Kena, G., Bianco, K., Frohlich, L., Kemp, J., & Tahan, K. (2011). *The condition of education 2011* (NCES 2011–033). Washington, DC: U.S. Department of Education, National Center for Education Statistics.

Blasé, J., & Roberts, J. (1994). The micropolitics of teacher work involvement: Effective principals' impacts on teachers. *Alberta Journal of Educational Research, 40*(1), 67–94.

Mann, H. (1848). 11th annual report to the Massachusetts State Board of Education. In Lawrence A. Cremin, (Ed.), *The republic and the school: Horace Mann on the education of free men* (pp. 79–97). New York, NY: Teachers College Press, 1957.

Orwell, G. (1945). *Animal farm*. Orlando, FL: Harcourt Brace.

Pew Research Foundation. (2011). *Wealth gaps rise to record high between whites, blacks, and Hispanics*. Retrieved from http://msnbcmedia.msn.com/i/msnbc/sections/news/Wealth_Report.pdf

Price, B. (2011). *Have public schools turned out to be "the great equalizer"*? Retrieved from http://www.freerepublic.com/focus/f-chat/2752429/posts

U.S. Department of Commerce. (2008). *Current Population Survey (CPS), annual social and economic supplement*. Washington, DC: Author.

U.S. Department of Education, National Center for Education Statistics. (n.d.). *Revenues and expenditures for public elementary and secondary education*. Washington, DC: Author.

Yudof, M., Levin, B., Moran, R., Ryan, J., & Bowman, K. (2012). *Educational policy and the law* (5th ed.). Belmont, CA: Wadsworth, Cengage Learning.

Zakaria, F. (2011, March 3). Are America's best days behind us? *Time*, p. 25.

Chapter 2

Boykin, W., & Noguera, P. (2011). *Creating the opportunity to learn: Moving from research to practice to close the achievement gap*. Alexandria, VA: ASCD.

Complete College America. (2012). *Remediation: Higher education's bridge to nowhere*. Retrieved from http://completecollege.org/docs/CCA-Remediation-final.pdf

Conley, D. (2011). *Creating college readiness*. Eugene, OR: Educational Policy Improvement Center. Retrieved from http://www.epiconline.org

Conley, D. (2012). *A complete definition of college and career readiness*. Eugene, OR: Educational Policy Improvement Center. Retrieved from http://www.epiconline.org

Council of Chief State School Officers & National Governors Association. (2012). *Common core standards webinar*. Retrieved from http://www.corestandards.org/resources

Delpit, L. (2012). *Multiplication is for White people: Raising expectations for other people's children*. New York, NY: New Press.

DeNavas-Walt, C., Proctor, B. D., & Smith, J. C. (2013). *Income, poverty, and health insurance coverage in the United States: 2012*. Current Population Reports. Washington, DC: U.S. Bureau of the Census.

Dweck, C. (2006). *Mindset: The new psychology of success*. New York, NY: Ballantine Books.

FRED Economic Research. (2014). *Unemployment rate—Not enrolled in school, high school graduates, no college, 16–24 years*. Retrieved from http://research.stlouisfed.org/fred2/series/LNU04023068?cid=32447

Fullan, M. (2013). *Stratosphere: Integrating technology, pedagogy, and change knowledge*. Toronto, Ontario, Canada: Pearson.

Haycock, K. (2005). *Good teaching matters: How well qualified teachers close the gap*. Retrieved from http://www.edtrust.org/dc/publication/good-teaching-matters-how-well-qualified-teachers-can-close-the-gap

Jennings, J. (2011). Have we gotten it wrong on school reform? *Huffington Post*. Retrieved from http://www.huffingtonpost.com/jack-jennings/school-reform-wrong_b_1110382.html

Johnson, L. B. (1964). *Public papers of U.S. presidents: Lyndon B. Johnson, 1963–1964* (1, 375–380). Washington, DC: U.S. Government Printing Office.

Kurlaender, M., & Howell, J. S. (2012). *Collegiate remediation: A review of the causes and consequences*. New York, NY: College Board.

National Assessment of Educational Progress. (2012). *2008 Long-term trend report card*. Retrieved from http://nationsreportcard.gov/ltt_2008/

National Commission on Excellence in Education. (1983). *A nation at risk: The imperative for education reform*. Retrieved from http://www2.ed.gov/pubs/NatAtRisk/index.html

Ogbu, J. (1992). Understanding cultural diversity and learning. *Educational Researcher, 21,* 8.

Stigler, J., & Hiebert, J. (1999). *The teaching gap: Best ideas from the world's teachers for improving education in the classroom*. New York, NY: Free Press.

U.S. Bureau of Labor Statistics. (2014). *The employment situation—March 2014*. Retrieved from http://www.bls.gov/news.release/pdf/empsit.pdf

Yeager, D., & Walton, G. (2011). Social-psychological interventions in education: They're not magic. *Review of Educational Research, 81,* 267–301.

Chapter 3

Bambrick-Santoyo, P. (2010). *Driven by data: A practical guide to improve instruction*. San Francisco, CA: Jossey-Bass.

Benevino, M., Snodgrass, D., Adams, K., & Dengel, J. (1999). *An educator's guide to block scheduling*. Needham Heights, MA: Allyn & Bacon.

Bernhardt, V. (2004). *Data analysis for continuous school improvement* (2nd ed.). Larchmont, NY: Eye on Education.

Bernhardt, V. (2008). *Data data everywhere: Bringing it all together for continuous improvement*. Larchmont, NY: Eye on Education.

Blythe, T., Allen, D., & Powell, B. (1999). *Looking together at student work*. New York, NY: Teachers College Press.

Boykin, W., & Noguera, P. (2011). *Creating the opportunity to learn: Moving from research to practice to close the achievement gap*. Alexandria, VA: ASCD.

Canady, R., & Rettig, M. (1995). School scheduling. *Educational Leadership, 53*(3), 4–10.

City, E., Elmore, R., Fiarman, S., & Teitel, L. (2009). *Instructional rounds in education: A network approach to improving teaching and learning*. Cambridge, MA: Harvard Education Press.

Croft, A., Coggshall, J., Dolan, M., Powers, E., & Killion, J. (2010, April). *Job-embedded professional development: What it is, who is responsible, and how to get it done well*. Retrieved from http://www.tqsource.org/publications/JEPD%20Issue%20Brief.PDF

Cuban, L., & Tyack, D. (1995). *Tinkering toward utopia: A century of public school reform*. Cambridge, MA: Harvard University Press.

Curtis, T., & Bidwell, W. (1977). *Curriculum and instruction for emerging adolescents*. Reading, MA: Addison-Wesley.

Darling-Hammond, L. (1996). *What matters most: Teaching for America's future*. Washington, DC: National Commission on Teaching and America's Future.

DuFour, R., Eaker, R., Karthanek, G., & DuFour, R. (2004). *Whatever it takes: How professional learning communities respond when kids don't learn*. Bloomington, IN: Solution Tree Press.

Ellis, A. (2001). *Teaching, learning, and assessment together: The reflective classroom*. Larchmont, NY: Eye on Education.

Elmore, R. (1997). Education policy and practice in the aftermath of TIMSS. In A. Beatty (Ed.), *Learning from TIMSS: Results of the Third International Mathematics and Science Study*. Washington, DC: National Academy Press.

Ferraro, J. (2000). *Reflective practice and professional development*. Washington, DC: ERIC Clearinghouse on Teaching and Teacher Education. (ERIC Document Reproduction Service No. ED 449120)

Fredricks, J. A., Blumenfeld, P. C., & Paris, A. H. (2004). School engagement: Potential of the concept, state of the evidence. *Review of Educational Research, 74*, 59–109.

Fullan, M. (1999). *Change forces: The sequel*. London, UK: Taylor & Francis/Falmer.

Fullan, M. (2001). *Leading in culture of change*. San Francisco, CA: Jossey-Bass.

Fullan, M. (2008). *The six secrets of change: What the best leaders do to help their organizations survive and thrive*. San Francisco, CA: Jossey-Bass.

Gill, B., Timpane, M., Ross, K., & Brewer, D. (2001). *Rhetoric versus reality: What we know and what we need to know about vouchers and charter schools*. Santa Monica, CA: RAND.

Guskey, T. (2000). *Evaluating professional development*. Thousand Oaks, CA: Corwin.

Guskey, T. (2002). Does it make a difference? Evaluating professional development. *Educational Leadership, 59*(6), 45–51.

Jensen, E. (2009). *Teaching with poverty in mind*. Alexandria, VA: ASCD.

Johnson, R. (2002). *Using data to close the achievement gap: How to measure equity in our schools*. Thousand Oaks, CA: Sage.

Kelley, J., & Shaw, J. (2009). *Learning first! A school leader's guide to closing achievement gaps*. Thousand Oaks, CA: Sage.

Krueger, R. A. (1988). *Focus groups: A practical guide for applied research*. Newbury Park, CA: Sage.

Marzano, R. (2003). *What works in schools: Translating research into action*. Alexandria, VA: ASCD.

Marzano, R., & Heflebower, T. (2001). *Teaching and assessing 21st century skills*. Bloomington, IN: Marzano Research Laboratory.

Marzano, R., & Pickering, D. with Heflebower, T. (2010). *The highly engaged classroom*. Bloomington, IN: Marzano Research Laboratory.

Nanus, B. (1992). *Visionary leadership: Creating a compelling sense of direction for your organization*. San Francisco, CA: Jossey-Bass.

Perelman, L. (1992). *School's out: Hyperlearning, the new technology, and the end of education*. New York, NY: William Morrow.

Phillips, V., & Olson, L. (2013). *Ensuring effective instruction: How do I improve teaching using multiple measures?* Alexandria, VA: ASCD.

Putnam, R., & Borko, H. (2000). What do new views of knowledge and thinking have to say about research on teacher learning? *Educational Researcher, 29*(1), 4–15.

Rocha, E. (2007). *Choosing more time for students: The what, why, and how of expanded learning*. Retrieved from http://www.americanprogress.org

Rosenshine, B. (1995). Advances in research on instruction. *Journal of Educational Research, 88*(5), 262–268.

Scheurich, J., & Skrla, L. (2003). *Leadership for equity and excellence: Creating high-achievement classrooms, schools, and districts*. Thousand Oaks, CA: Sage.

Sergiovanni, T. J. (1990). Adding value to leadership gets extraordinary results. *Educational Leadership, 47*(8), 23–27.

Spear, R. (1992). Middle level team scheduling: Appropriate grouping for adolescents. *Schools in the Middle, 2*(1), 30–34.

U.S. Census Bureau. (2008). *An older and more diverse nation by midcentury.* Retrieved from http://www.census.gov/newsroom/releases/archives/population/cb08-123.html

U.S. Bureau of the Census. (2010). *2010 U.S. Census.* Retrieved from http://www.census.gov/2010census/

U.S. Department of Education, National Archives and Records Administration. (2009). Department of Education, State Fiscal Stabilization Fund program: Final rule. *Federal Register, 74*(217), 58479–58525. Retrieved from http://www.nsdc.org/standards/

Wellman, B., & Lipton, L. (2004). *Data-driven dialogue: A facilitator's guide to collaborative inquiry.* Sherman, CT: MiraVia.

Chapter 4

Bitters, B. A. (1999). *Useful definitions for exploring education equity.* Madison: Wisconsin Department of Public Instruction, Equity Mission Team.

Costa, A., & Garmston, R. (2002). *Cognitive coaching: A foundation for renaissance schools.* Norwood, MA: Christopher-Gordon.

Ferguson, R. F. (1991). Paying for public education: New evidence on how and why money matters. *Harvard Journal on Legislation, 28,* 465–499.

Ferguson, R. F. (1998). Teachers' perceptions and expectations and the black-white test score gap. In C. Jencks & M. Phillips (Eds.), *The black-white test score gap* (pp.273–317). Washington, DC: Brookings Institution.

Kincheloe, J. L. (2004). Why a book on urban education? In S. Steinberg & J. Kincheloe (Eds.), *19 urban questions: Teaching in the city* (pp.1–32). New York, NY: Peter Lang.

Kincheloe, J. L. (2010). Why a book on urban education? In S. Steinberg (Ed.), *19 urban questions: Teaching in the city* (2nd ed., pp.1–28). New York, NY: Peter Lang.

Leithwood, K., & Riehl, C. (2003). *What we know about successful school leadership.* Manchester, UK: National College for School Leadership. Retrieved from http://www.principals.in/uploads/pdf/leadership/1_NCLP.pdf

Souba, W. (2007). The leadership dilemma. *Journal of Surgical Research, 138,* 1–9.

Stanford Educational Leadership Institute. (2007). *Preparing school leaders for a changing world: Lessons from exemplary leadership development programs.* Retrieved from http://seli.stanford.edu

Wallace Foundation. (2008). *Becoming a leader: Preparing school principals for today's schools.* Retrieved from http://www.wallacefoundation.org/knowledge-center/school-leadership/principal-training/Pages/Becoming-a-Leader-Preparing-Principals-for-Todays-Schools.aspx

Chapter 5

Bambrick-Santoyo, P. (2010). *Driven by data: A practical guide to improve instruction.* San Francisco, CA: Jossey-Bass.

Bellanca, J., & Rodriguez, E. R. (2007). *What is it about me you can't teach? An instructional guide for the urban educator.* Thousand Oaks, CA: Corwin.

Boudett, K. P., & Steele, J. (2007). *Data wise in action*. Cambridge, MA: Harvard Education Press.

Boykin, W., & Noguera, P. (2011). *Creating the opportunity to learn: Moving from research to practice to close the achievement gap*. Alexandria, VA: ASCD.

Cushman, K., & Delpit, L. (2003). *Fires in the bathroom: Advice for teachers from high school students*. New York, NY: New Press.

Jerald, C., Haycock, K., & Wilkens, A. (2009). *Fighting for quality and equality, too: How state policymakers can ensure the drive to improve teacher quality doesn't just trickle down to poor and minority children*. Retrieved from http://www.edtrust.org/sites/edtrust.org/files/publications/files/QualityEquality

Johnson, R. (2002). *Using data to close the achievement gap: How to measure equity in our schools*. Thousand Oaks, CA: Corwin.

Johnson, R., & LaSalle, R. (2010). *Data strategies to uncover and eliminate hidden inequities*. Thousand Oaks, CA: Corwin.

Kelly, C., & Shaw, J. (2009). *Learning first: A school leader's guide to closing achievement gaps*. Thousand Oaks, CA: Corwin.

Ladson-Billings, G. (1995). But that's just good teaching! The case for culturally relevant pedagogy. *Theory into Practice, 34*(3), 159–165.

Ladson-Billings, G. (2009). *The dream keepers*. San Francisco, CA: Jossey-Bass.

Lemov, D. (2010). *Teach like a champion*. San Francisco, CA: Jossey-Bass.

National Education Association. (2013). *Why cultural competence?* Retrieved from http://www.nea.org/home/39783.htm

Pink, D. (1995). *Drive: The surprising truth about what motivates us*. New York, NY: Penguin.

Stigler, J., & Hiebert, J. (1999). *The teaching gap*. New York: Free Press.

Tatum, A. (2005). *Teaching reading to black adolescent males*. Portland, ME: Stenhouse.

Chapter 6

Fullan, M. (2001). *Leading in a culture of change*. San Francisco, CA: Jossey-Bass.

Fullan, M. (2008). *The six secrets of change: What the best leaders do to help their organizations survive and thrive*. San Francisco, CA: Jossey-Bass.

Kotter, J. (1996). *Leading change: An action plan from the world's foremost expert on business leadership*. Boston, MA: Harvard Business School Press.

Reeves, D. (2010). *Transforming professional development into student results*. Alexandria, VA: ASCD.

Chapter 7

Carter, P., & Weiner, G. (2013). *Closing the opportunity gap: What America must do to give every child an even chance*. New York, NY: Oxford University Press.

Fullan, M. (2011). *Change leader: Learning to do what matters most*. San Francisco, CA: Jossey-Bass.

Govindarajan, V., & Trimble, C. (2010). *The other side of innovation: Solving the execution challenge*. Boston, MA: Harvard Business School Press.

Johnson, R., & LaSalle, R. (2010). *Data strategies to uncover and eliminate hidden inequities*. Thousand Oaks, CA: Corwin.

Kotter, J. (2011). *Change management vs. change leadership—What's the difference?* Retrieved from http://www.forbes.com/sites/johnkotter/2011/07/12/change-management-vs-change-leadership-whats-the-difference/

Wagner, T. (2012). *Creating innovators: The making of young people who will change the world.* New York, NY: Scribner's/Simon & Schuster.

Index

A SAGE Company

Corwin is committed to improving education for all learners by publishing books and other professional development resources for those serving the field of PreK–12 education. By providing practical, hands-on materials, Corwin continues to carry out the promise of its motto: **"Helping Educators Do Their Work Better."**